GET YOUR SHIFT TOGETHER

GET YOUR

SHIFT

TOGETHER

How to Take Control
of Your Health and Finances
and Achieve Your Dream Life

Kimberly LeGrand

HEALTH CREATES HAPPINESS

ISBN: 978-0-578-97981-6

Published by Health Creates Happiness

Cover and interior page design and layout
by Stephen Tiano, Book Designer of Riverhead, NY
stephen@stephentianobookdesign.com

Printed in the United States of America

I dedicate this book to my parents for their support of my ever-evolving interests and for always being the guinea pigs for my bizarre healthy twists on recipes; to my husband for encouraging me to pursue my passions; to the authors, speakers, researchers, and educators for thinking outside the box and being brave enough to share their knowledge with the world.

Contents

Introduction

My aim with this book is to support you in getting your "shift" together when it comes to your health and finances. This means making shifts to take you from point A (now) to point B (wherever you want to be.) These shifts are not extreme movements, but rather small, incremental changes in direction, where ultimately, you are pointing straight toward your point B, your dream life.

People may work on both their health and personal finances their entire lives but never really get to where they want to be. Maybe you've already been at it for several years without much progress. It can be discouraging, right? I am here to tell you it doesn't have to be that way! This life you're living is yours. You have the power to create whatever you want. So, pat yourself on the back for not giving up on your goals, and get ready to start the shift toward them.

I've been in bad places with my weight, confidence, how I was treating my body, and also my attitude toward money. Over time, I've pulled myself out of these dark pits and found ways to maintain good physical and financial health. I want to emphasize this happened "over time." The shifts in my life didn't happen overnight, and yours won't either. Everything in this book is aimed at achieving what you want for yourself, but more importantly, lifetime maintenance of these things. I don't care about speed and I'm not satisfied with just a short-term vision. Short-term thinking is not the way to succeed.

This book doesn't get into the science and super specific plans behind healthy living. It focuses on a shift in mindset—to living heathy, to get rid of the confusion that exists around what changes to make and to find an approach that truly works for you. Everyone needs something a little different based on where they are today, where they want to go, what they enjoy in life, and other individual circumstances. But everyone can work on mindset first and then strategy will follow.

I've struggled with aspects of my own health, spent many years learning about different perspectives on health and well-being, and a lot of time working on my mindset and emotional health. Having a generally healthy life can be so simple; I want to keep things as easy as possible and give you hope that you can achieve whatever you desire without completely changing your current lifestyle.

This book doesn't get into the intricacies of a full financial plan for your future or how to invest. This book lays out a plan to get a handle on your financial situation; know exactly what you make and what you spend (your personal income statement), make some decisions about how you can adjust that, and turn your relationship with your finances from stressful and worrisome to peaceful and fun. Many people do not yet have these foundational concepts in place, so that's what this book addresses.

We humans complicate things thanks to our complex, fascinating, and frustrating minds.

I've followed some fairly basic financial principles for many years to put myself in a good position for the future. I'm also a CPA, so I have an innate love for numbers. Of course, it hasn't been a straight line; I have had highs and lows with my relationship with money and I'll talk more about that. My goal in this book is to support you in feeling like you're in control of your financial situation. The majority of people can take what they currently earn and make better use of it. And no, it doesn't need to take a lot of time. For whatever reason, many just do not carve out a bit of time to understand and work on their finances. Trust me, a little effort goes a long way. We will start working on that today!

Money and health are my two passions. It feels right to talk about both in the same book, even if that seems strange at first. Maybe you feel like you need more support in one area than the other, or maybe you feel like one of the areas isn't of concern at all. No matter what your thoughts are today, I encourage you to read the whole book and reflect on all the topics and questions I pose. You may be surprised that you learn something new about yourself. There could be something lurking in your mind, deep down in the abyss of your subconscious, that is holding you back. Now's the time to find it, say hello to it, and then kick it to the curb.

Before we get into the first chapter, I want to say something about timing. We often hear the phrase "timing is everything." This can and does apply to many things in life, including taking action as you read this book. When it comes to making changes in your daily habits, it's tough. Obviously, it's tough or everyone would be exactly where they want to be. When you have specific circumstances and a purpose driving you to make a change, it's easier to say yes to new habits. You may have tried to make certain changes in the past, maybe multiple times, without success. Forget about that. Today is a new day. Start fresh. The past doesn't have to predict the future. You can do anything. Start to believe that right now.

Grab a pen and notebook and get ready to shift!

CHAPTER ONE

What's the Big Deal?

Why do we care about the subjects of health and money? What's the big deal about them? Why are they important to so many of us, yet so hard to get a handle on?

Let's start with health. The big deal is that good health can open up your life to so many possibilities, or it can make life feel very small if it's bad. Good health means being able to travel, be active, play with your kids, wake up with energy, have a strong, clear mind, and handle stress. Poor health means being uncomfortable on a regular basis, not feeling well enough to exercise, sleeping poorly, having low energy, depression, brain fog, or a weak immune system. Which of these scenarios sounds more appealing?

The big deal about personal finances is that those finances should get you through all the phases of your life, including retirement, and maybe even carry on as part of your legacy after you've passed away. Unless you're willing to find a remote island somewhere and literally live off the land, you need money to get through life. There's no escaping it. How much money depends on the individual, but we all need some.

Why have I put these two subjects together in one book?

I believe that if you're struggling in one area of your life, you're likely struggling in other areas of your life for the *exact same reasons!* Our habits around food, money, relationships, exercise, etc., impact not just one facet of life, but all of them. So, let's tackle everything in one fell swoop.

If you make improvements in "inconsequential" areas, you'll see improvements in so many other aspects of your life.

It may be that you feel like life is great *except* for those extra pounds you're carrying, or except for those aches and pains that seem to get worse and more numerous, or except for the digestive issues you're dealing with, or except for the daily fatigue, or except for the fact that you're getting more and more into debt, or except for the fact that you're constantly worrying about whether you'll ever be able to retire . . . know that these things that seem isolated, aren't. I assure you, if you make improvements in these "inconsequential" areas, you'll see improvements in so many other aspects of your life. You'll give yourself the opportunity to level up your life and get closer to achieving what you were put on this planet for.

Health is critical to *everything*. When you feel like crap, you're not going to perform well in life. The way you show up as a business person, parent, and friend won't be optimal. And if you're so unhealthy that you don't just feel bad, but you're actually limited in physical movement, the ability to work, or the ability to be around other people, now we are talking about a significant issue.

Financial stability is also critical to *everything*. I'm not talking about making a million bucks (although that's totally possible for everyone), but just being responsible with the money you are currently earning; figuring out how to make your money get you through life now, *plus* how to start saving for the future. Despite how much it sometimes feels like the problem is not making enough money, for the vast majority of people, it's not. In most cases, you can work with your current income and make ends meet while also saving. Maybe in this process you'll identify an opportunity to make more money as well. But let's start with the basics of managing what you've got now. If you don't learn some money management skills, you'll always be in the same situation, regardless of how much you make.

There's no magic formula, there's no secret trick or potion to making changes in your life. It takes daily action. It's the small, seemingly inconsequential decisions every single day that add up to the results you've always wanted. Darren Hardy, a successful entrepreneur, international bestselling author, speaker, publisher, and success mentor, details this concept in *The Compound Effect*. I highly recommend his fantastic book. No magic; just action! And honestly, it's so simple. I can't stress that enough. Simplicity can be misleading. We all think things need to be complicated to be effective. Or, when things are simple, we clever humans tend to get bored with them. Hence, we jump into different diet plans, workout plans, money strategies; we want different cars or clothes or phones, or even different relationships. Get that out of your head! Simple is great when it comes to the foundational principles for having a kick-ass life. Simple may not be very sexy, but the results are.

When you get the simple stuff working like clockwork, then being healthy and financially stable don't require any effort. You can spend your time doing truly fun things and having life adventures. Also, the changes discussed in this book don't cost anything. You know my frugal, cost-conscious CPA brain loves that!

Let's get clear right now that you are in charge of the results you get. The fact that your daily decisions can help you with any change you want to make is an amazing thing. You have the power. You hold the key. I realize this may feel overwhelming or depressing if you don't trust yourself. If you're feeling that way, acknowledge that feeling, put it aside for now, and keep reading. We'll work on this together.

If anything came super easy to us, it wouldn't be meaningful. That might get an eye roll from you, but just stay with me. This is all about behavioral changes, which aren't easy. Behaviors take years to form, so it's not as easy as flipping a switch to shift behavior. You may already know this because you've tried a dozen times to change habits and haven't had long-term success. The good news is that none of the actions required are hard—they take discipline, yes, but they're not hard. If you can change your thoughts, you can change your life.

The question is, How long are you willing to let those old habits hold you back from getting to a place in life that truly makes you happy; where you have *space* to get creative, feel alive, get in touch with your true self, and live your best life? I emphasize the word *space* because it's really important, and for a long time, I legitimately hated that word, but we'll talk more about that later.

Are you willing to let another six months go by without making progress toward your goals? A year? Five years? Ten years? That may sound dramatic but it's not an exaggeration. I've been there, letting things just glide along for years at a time, knowing that I really wanted to change and achieve different things (like writing a book), but never getting the job done. Let's stop that today. You deserve better.

I've got to throw in a small plea from a parent's perspective. Even if you're not a parent, maybe you're around little humans in some capacity. Kids are always watching and learning from the people they spend time with. What kind of example do you want to set? Do you want to demonstrate a healthy relationship with food and exercise? Do you want to demonstrate a healthy attitude toward finances? Yes, and yes! Of course, you and I both want the best for the little humans in our lives, and this is a great reason to live out the principles discussed here.

Chapter Summary

1. Getting your health in order and your finances on track bring peace of mind.
2. Health is the driver of your life. If your health is fantastic, possibilities are endless. If your health is suffering, everything else in life is more challenging.
3. Personal financial stability allows you to focus on other areas of life that bring you joy instead of stressing about paying the bills.
4. YOU have the choice to take control of both areas in life. YOU can create your dream life.

CHAPTER TWO

The Connection Between Money and Health

Health and personal finances are two areas the vast majority of people worry about. Would you agree with that? Worry leads to stress, which leads to anxiety, then to unhappy feelings and relationships, emotional eating and emotional spending, and all kinds of bad habits. You get the idea.

I want to talk about stress. Stress is a fascinating subject. The dictionary definition of stress is "a state of mental or emotional strain or tension resulting from adverse or very demanding circumstances." That's pretty straightforward.

We all have stress in our lives. You may be like me and vehemently work to rid yourself of any stress-inducing activities, but you've probably learned that it's impossible. You may be someone who is so used to high stress levels that it just feels like normal life. I was that person once.

Stress is a part of life in some way, shape, or form. That's okay! Stress is actually a survival mechanism (fight or flight), so we don't want to get rid of it all together. But when we get ourselves in a situation where stress is occurring too often, even when there isn't a true threat, that's when it takes a toll on us.

Stress is sometimes called the silent killer. When a situation presents itself that causes stress, our body braces itself to react. It may tense up, the mind becomes focused, breathing quickens, and the nervous system goes into overdrive. During this preparation for battle, the body also suppresses the immune and reproductive systems while flooding the liver with extra blood sugar. If there is danger, this reaction is a good thing. If there is no danger, the result is unnecessary wear and tear on the body. Both physical and mental well-being take a hit when the body's reactions don't match the situation.

When unnecessary stress becomes the norm, your body's systems become overtaxed and stop working as they should. This chronic stress slowly eats away at your health, presenting itself in a host of different ways. The overt symptoms could be things like mood changes, headaches, heartburn, upset stomach, decreased sex drive, missed periods in women, or rapid breathing. Would you necessarily attribute these things to stress? Not likely. Less obvious symptoms could be things like an increased risk of heart attack, a weakened immune system, or high blood pressure. That's why stress is called the silent killer. Stress, if it becomes chronic, can screw up your entire system.

I went through a few years of chronic stress, primarily due to work. Irritability and the reluctance to socialize were the most profound symptoms I experienced. I'm an introvert, so not always wanting to socialize is normal for me. However, it was amplified during this period of stress. Sometimes the thought of having to engage in casual conversation, even with friends and family, was too much for me to handle. Talk about a sad time. I also experienced significant digestive discomfort to the point of diagnosing myself as suffering from irritable bowel syndrome (IBS). Maybe I did have it, maybe not. Either way, stress was negatively impacting my health.

In terms of focusing on health and finances, let's work on reducing unnecessary stress from worrying about these issues, and leave stress for other stuff in life!

Health concerns can be: losing weight, lack of sleep, lack of concentration, aging, being out of shape, chronic pain, illness, genetic tendencies, not knowing what to eat, and so on. Money concerns can be: never having enough money, planning for retirement, supporting your family, not having a saving plan, credit card debt, student loans, overall cost of living, and even just the general keeping-up-with-the-Jones's mindset.

When you're concerned about financial matters, you may be stressed, overeat, suffer from insomnia, experience depression ... these all impact your health.

These can be heavy topics—they weigh on our mind day in and day out and cause stress. These are things that we lose sleep over. These can also be intimately related.

Think for a moment about some of the side effects you experience when dealing with money worries. When you're concerned about financial matters, what happens to you? You may feel stressed, overeat or make poor nutritional choices, suffer from insomnia, feel unmotivated to exercise, experience depression, personal relationships suffer, and the list goes on. These *all* impact your health.

Let's also think for a moment about possible side effects from health issues that could impact your financial well-being. You may have extra medical bills, miss work more than you'd like to which prevents you from getting that promotion, not be able to perform well at your job (whether that's due to concentration, focus, alertness, attitude, or anything else) causing you to miss out on bonus opportunities, spend more money dining out, and spend more money on other things just because you aren't happy. Money can be an emotional outlet; we will dive into that more a little bit later.

Can you see how these two topics are intertwined? Can you see how when you're suffering in one area, it can impact the other area; therefore, when you start to heal one area, you can start to heal the other? It all goes back to habits. Habits with your health carry over to habits with money and vice versa. If you can set good habits in one area, they can help you in all areas of life.

Chapter Summary
1. Stress surrounding your health impacts your finances: more healthcare expenses, lower level of performance in your job/business, emotional spending.
2. Stress surrounding your finances impacts your health: anxiety, inability to sleep, lack of motivation to exercise.
3. If you can make improvements in one of these two areas, the other will improve!

CHAPTER THREE

It's Not Punishment, It's Freedom

Healthy eating, exercise, and saving money aren't forms of punishment. You've got to stop thinking of them that way. Mel Robbins, a well-known speaker and author, says something along the lines of "Change your mindset, change your life." This is so simple and so true. Start changing your language around these topics today.

I repeatedly hear people say that they "deserve" to eat pizza, chocolate, ice cream, fries, etc., "deserve" to take a break from exercise, or "deserve" to spend money on whatever they feel like. Trust me, I'm familiar with these justifications. It's comfortable. It's easy. And sometimes you truly believe that these thoughts are accurate. You tell yourself *I've worked really hard today,* or *I've handled a lot of stressful situations today,* or *My kids have been driving me crazy today, therefore I deserve* _____. I fully understand the sentiment behind these thoughts, but this is where your mindset must change. These are the thoughts that hold you back from getting all the juiciness you want out of your life.

Start looking at the new habits you're working to form as awesome. View them as supporting the amazing life you know you want for yourself. *That's* what you deserve.

Let's take the example of deciding whether or not to make a spur-of-the-moment purchase. A cute shirt caught your eye in a store and you feel giddiness bubbling up inside of you at the prospect of taking it home. In that moment, you want the emotional high of buying the shirt. You also know that you have a ton of shirts in your closet already and your ultimate financial goal is saving money to buy a house. Just this once, don't buy the shirt. It feels like a punishment in that moment the first time you make that decision. But if you repeat this same decision multiple times, it gets easier and ultimately gives you freedom! Freedom from the regret that often ensues after doing something that doesn't support your goals... again. Freedom to trust yourself. Freedom in recognizing your emotions and how they're impacting your decisions. The long-term freedom you gain far outweighs the short-term pleasure you enjoy from an impulse buy.

Freedom to Create your Future

There are countless money decisions that come up every single day. Each of these decisions matters to your overall goals. Sure, it's easier to go about your day and not think twice about spending money or how much something costs. It may feel like a lot of pressure or an extra burden to start thinking about each purchase you make. It can be at first—it can feel like a total drag. But that is short-lived. Do this for a week and see how much easier it gets in that time frame. Do this for a month and you'll find it becomes second nature, not burdensome, and saves you from spending money on things that you won't miss.

The difference between paying attention to each purchase versus not doing so is the critical difference between improving your cash flow and the ability to save or not. This should make you extremely excited to start this practice. Again, this is going to give you freedom!

Taking a look at the health side of your decisions, unhealthy food increases toxins, disrupts your digestive system, impairs your cognitive thinking, spikes your blood sugar, causes weight gain, and impairs your immune system, among many other things. Keeping this in the forefront of your mind will help you make better decisions. I get it, greasy fries taste amazing. Biting into a decadent chocolate cake feels like Christmas. So, sure, these foods give you a short-term emotional high because they taste good going in. The negative impacts, though, both short-term (lethargy, upset stomach) and long-term (weight gain, disease) don't come close to making the short-term emotional high worth it.

The world loses millions of people every year to lifestyle diseases: heart disease, diabetes, metabolic syndrome, some types of cancer, liver disease, and so on. When I say *lifestyle diseases*, I mean the negative health consequences of daily habits that result from one's own actions. I heard a nutritionist describe these as *diseases of dietary excess*.

Each time you choose to eat or drink something you know isn't going to support your health goals, it contributes to the potential of developing a lifestyle disease. Isn't it more of a punishment to put junk in your body than it is to make even just a slightly healthier choice in what you're eating?

Freedom to Feel your Best

Even people who aren't overweight can suffer from lifestyle diseases. Weight is not always an indicator of a person's health. Absent serious medical conditions, getting to the point of being overweight or suffering from other nutrition-related ailments is due to the choices we make on a daily basis. You choose not to hang out with sick people because you don't want to get sick. So, choose not to eat low-nutrient foods because they make you sick. It's the same thing, except eating low-nutrient or processed food on a consistent basis is actually worse than getting the flu; the flu is usually a temporary unpleasant experience. Even if you have an awful flu, you'll suffer for a week or two and then you'll recover and feel healthy again. But consistently eating foods void of nutrients can make you ill and uncomfortable for a long time and end your life prematurely.

We are meant to live a long life and then die quickly. When we bring in lifestyle diseases, we still may live a long life, but we die a much slower death

---

A doctor was interviewed as part of a video series on reversing diabetes, and what he said really stuck with me: we are meant to live a long life and then die quickly; that's what most species do. However, when we bring in lifestyle diseases, this can mean that we still live a long(ish) life, but we die a much slower death over many years as our bodies deteriorate from all the junk we put in them. This isn't a game. This is your life! It's vitally important that you take care of yourself to the best of your ability.

Health is easily taken for granted when you have it. Then, when it's taken away, even by a cold or sore throat (when all of a sudden you can't swallow even a sip of water without agony), you realize how darn good it is.

The most serious health concern I've faced so far in my life was skin cancer. I had a Mohs procedure on my nose to get rid of basal cell carcinoma followed by a six-week topical treatment to target any remaining problem areas. The topical treatment was far worse than the surgery, if you can believe it, due to the daily emotional impact. Sadness crept up each time I looked in the mirror and saw the nasty scabs forming on my face. Fear would come and go as my mind drifted down all kinds of rabbit holes thinking about how many more bouts of skin cancer I might deal with over the course of my life, worst case scenarios, the potential of having permanent scars on my face, and getting angry at myself for not having done more to prevent being in this position in the first place. I cried some big, ugly tears. That was the first time I ever truly considered my own death. Crazy, right? I pictured my baby girl growing up without a mother and it was too much to bear. That was a rough time for me, and in those moments, I viewed my health as something much bigger than having six-pack abs or a cellulite-free rear end. I couldn't care less about my physique during that time.

The point of sharing this personal experience is to show that all health scares, no matter the size, take away from enjoying life. Being in good health is such a gift and you have the power to support your body in giving you just that; you also have the power to put a lot of strain on your body and make it work hard to stay healthy. The choice is yours. If you can shift your mindset and think about your health in this way, it will support you to make decisions that lead to you living your best life rather than constantly taxing your body.

The mental clarity you gain from good nutrition is enough of a benefit, in my view, to make all the changes and short-term sacrifices worth it. If I could give people a glimpse—even if just for a few hours—of how their cognition improves with proper nutrition, I'm sure many more people would make changes and stick to them. Think about getting rid of brain fog and those awful afternoon yawns making you want a catnap at your desk to survive the day. Think about your memory working optimally. Think about having quick responses in conversations. Think about better decision-making. Make better food choices and you can support your body in achieving these things.

Freedom to Change your Thoughts

Number one *New York Times* bestselling author and spiritual teacher Eckhart Tolle said, "Be at least as interested in what goes on inside as what happens outside. If you get the inside right, the outside will fall into place." This made such an impact on me. When I talk about humans already knowing the things we are "supposed to" do to be healthy or to improve our financial situation—but for some dang reason not being able to stick to those habit changes—this quote fits right in. We can't just focus on the outside; how our hair looks, how we fit into those skinny jeans or bathing suit, how up-to-date our wardrobe is, how big our house is, or how much money we have in the bank. We've got to pay attention to the inside; our thoughts, mindset, and emotions. We will dive into this more throughout the book.

> **Be at least as interested in what goes on inside as what happens outside. If you get the inside right, the outside will fall into place.**
> **—ECKHART TOLLE**

If you pay attention to how you're feeling when you eat certain foods, you'll get better at making good decisions in the heat of the moment. If you notice eating a gluttonous meal makes you feel lethargic, the next time you're faced with a food decision (say, at a business lunch) think about how you want to feel after your meeting when you have to go back to the office and work for the rest of the day. If feeling lethargic at work is A-OK, then go for the fatty meal. If that's not your ideal work scenario, choose something lighter and more balanced. For me, pushing through the afternoon energy crash that comes from overeating is horrible. I can remember times when I've had to stand up at my desk and literally hold my eyelids open to stay awake. I get plenty of sleep, so this kind of energy crash is definitely food related.

When you make these connections—identifying which foods make you feel great and which foods make you feel terrible, you can start to shift your mindset away from the typical thoughts of "good" versus "bad" foods. Many people look at things like pizza or cookies as "bad" foods and then at a plate of chicken and roasted vegetables as "good" foods. We've been trained to look at food this way through years of media exposure, nutrition articles, and so on. I understand the sentiment behind this thought process. It comes from a reasonable place; looking at how nutrient-dense or how processed each food is and what other ingredients are added to the food during preparation (like sugar). I agree that looking at these things is all part of deciding which foods have the most to offer your body. However, I don't think it's mentally beneficial to have a rigid sense of good foods and bad foods. I truly think you can eat any food you want, in moderation, as part of a healthy diet.

It is health that is real wealth and not pieces of gold and silver.
—GANDHI

Let's talk about spending and saving habits here too. It can feel uncomfortable or disappointing at first when you cut back on discretionary spending and add to your savings plan. Each day that you make a choice to *not* buy something you otherwise would have, you get stronger. You'll experience the joy of knowing you took a step in the right direction. You may later reflect on whatever you didn't buy and think about how inconsequential that item was to your life. You'll learn more about your own emotions and how temporary they can be. Trust me when I say that you'll also love the feeling you get from seeing a growing savings account!

As humans, there's something in our brains that makes us want things that we think are off limits. Sunday you tell yourself *I'm not eating any sugar for the next three days.* When you wake up Monday, what are you going to think about all day? Sugar! Even if your body isn't physically craving sugar, simply because you've told yourself it's off limits, your mind focuses on that. I'm sure you've experienced this phenomenon. Therefore, if we go through life with this automatic system of rating foods as good or bad, the mind naturally leads us to want the bad foods more often than we might otherwise actually crave them. Also, and maybe even more importantly, this system of good and bad foods leads to negative emotions. Every time you eat, you may end up feeling guilt, shame, or self-loathing. Trust me, there have been plenty of moments in my life where I've hidden food so that nobody would see what "bad" food I'd eaten. It makes you feel terrible and what's the purpose of that anyway? For me, it was to keep up my image of being a healthy eater and trying to be perfect. But at the end of the day, if you ate something, you ate something ... whether anybody else knows it or not. Hiding from the truth is exhausting and mentally unhealthy.

Eating food is part of life. It's part of survival, so it isn't going away. And it's supposed to be enjoyable, not just in the moment, but also afterward when you feel satisfied and energized. If you can get to a point where you think more about how foods make you *feel*, you'll start to let your mind work in your favor, rather than against you. And you can let go of guilt. That's no way to live.

One point I'd like to make is that there's definitely something magical when you make your own food. You develop a connection with it. You appreciate the food and the nutrition it's providing you. This can make you *want* to eat wholesome, real foods, rather than processed stuff. Also, if you're like me, you hate throwing away food. So, if you buy fresh ingredients and do some meal preparation, you must eat it before it goes bad. When the choice comes up to eat at home or go grab something quick and there's food in the fridge that needs to be eaten, well, my decision is made. Works like a charm.

Freedom to Replace Financial Stress with Fun
The biggest gain in taking control of your personal financial situation is reducing stress. Even a small amount of planning and effort getting a system in place to deal with your money can change your life. Getting rid of the worry that goes along with money immediately decreases your blood pressure, makes you a more joyful human being, and frees your mind to focus on other (more fun!) things in life. You'll gain confidence because you understand your personal financial situation, and happiness as you give yourself the chance to think positively about your future. Isn't that worth a small amount of your time?

I mentioned having *space* in Chapter 1. The first time I heard about "creating space" in my life, I was at a retreat for new entrepreneurs. It didn't make sense to me at first, but let me tell you, it has a lot of power when you understand the concept.

Let's think about the mind and how many things we have swirling around in there on a daily basis. Yes, our minds are incredible, intricate, amazing things and were built to handle a lot. But they, too, can be overloaded or overwhelmed. This makes me think about an episode of the sitcom *Married with Children*, where the daughter Kelly goes on a sports trivia game show. If you are familiar with the character and the TV show, you'll know she was a cute, fun, blond, but was not the sharpest tool in the shed. Her father, Al, didn't qualify for the show due to lack of personality, so he had Kelly try out in his place. In order to prep Kelly to be on this game show, Al "transferred" all of his sports knowledge to her but discovered that for each fact that went into her brain, another one fell out. Just before the game show began, she ends up learning one more new piece of information, not intended to be trivia knowledge. Fast forward to the end of the trivia show and Kelly was doing amazingly well. The answer to the last question was something she should've known based on her dad's brain dump of sports facts, but all she could come up with was the most recent thing she had learned (just prior to starting the trivia game). Her brain was at 100 percent capacity, so that one new piece of knowledge kicked another bit of actual sports knowledge right out of her head. I realize this is exaggerated and not reality, but it demonstrates my point: Our beautiful, complex brains get pretty darn full of everything we think about and learn and try to remember.

As a real-life example of the concept of mental space, I've heard that Barack Obama wore either a blue or gray suit every day while in office and that Mark Zuckerberg does something similar, but with a gray T-shirt. Why? It's one less decision to make each day. Both of these men have big responsibilities, along with daily problem-solving and decision-making. Removing this one morning decision saves time and mental space or energy.

Does this sound extreme? Maybe you and I aren't in the same position as a president of a country or CEO of a public company, and we don't have quite as many decisions to make every day. And maybe the decisions we make don't impact many people, but we still have full, busy lives. We still have important decisions to make that impact our own lives and the lives of our colleagues and families. I will not downplay the importance of those decisions for one second; the decisions we make on a daily basis are important. In fact, these are the decisions that I've referred to already in this book, ones that can feel small in the moment but eventually add up to something impactful. And these small decisions, over time, can result in exactly what we've envisioned for ourselves in terms of the life we want, or can result in something very far away from the life we truly want.

The more I can rely on autopilot for decisions in my life, the more mental space I create for creativity, fun, and handling unexpected twists that life throws my way. Generally speaking, I have a fairly steady pattern for all of my meals. I also have a set schedule for my workouts. Financially, I have habitual spending and saving patterns as well.

These habits have taken time to put in place, but now that I have them, they're easy. They don't require mental space because I don't even think about them. They're part of the flow of my day, just like brushing my teeth.

I know that starting out on a new journey to better health, a better financial situation, or anything else that you want to change takes effort. You have to put in effort; thinking, planning, and decision-making constantly. It can feel overwhelming and you think: *How on earth can I keep this up? How can I possibly make all these decisions every day, do all this planning, and keep up with the rest of the things going on in my life?* Doing things the old way, even if it's making you unhappy, is so much simpler. That's why it's easy to fall back into old habits quickly—it doesn't require thought.

When your mind starts telling you that it's too hard to take on new challenges, you've got to push through and keep going. Keep trudging up the hill. Don't roll back down to where you started. Keep moving and get yourself to the first peak. Once you get through this first "hard" period, effort, thinking, and planning come naturally and are so much easier. That's where you want to be.

Taking a close look at your money situation and your personal health are not punishments. By following some basic steps and getting a few mindset shifts started, you can unlock freedom you never knew existed and be rewarded with a new level of greatness in your life.

Chapter Summary
1. View your new health and finance habits as keys to your best life, not punishments.
2. Think about what you will gain rather than what you are giving up.
3. By changing your habits, you are gaining freedom: freedom to create the life you want, to feel your best, to change your thoughts, and to replace stress with fun. Yes, I said FUN. Life should be fun!

CHAPTER FOUR

Who Do You Want to Be?

Before we get into the strategy of changing your health and personal finance habits, I need to have an important conversation with you. I want you to think about who you want to be. This is your chance for some amazing self-reflection. This chapter is key in envisioning the life you want (your point B) so you can create a plan to get there. We don't often give ourselves time to just stop and think. We are good at rushing from one task to the next, checking things off the to-do list and trying to keep our heads on straight. Who has time to stop and think? Who has the luxury to reflect on life and where we are heading? Does that feel a little self-indulgent to you? That is precious time being wasted, right?

But those times of reflection, if we allow them, are so enlightening. If you've never done this, it's hard to wrap your head around the concept, but don't discount it. I'd never really thought about it prior to a women's leadership course I participated in. As part of this course, I spent a full 24 hours by myself, in an unfamiliar, but safe, location. I had no technology, no music, no books to take my mind to another place, and no other typical worldly distractions. It was just me and my thoughts, and let me tell you, it was quite the experience.

For the first part of this period, I just wondered exactly what I was going to do by myself for 24 hours. My mind wandered. I took a nap. I drank some water. I listened to the birds chirping in the trees. I listened to the cows mooing in a field nearby. I laid down and soaked up the sunshine. I took another nap.

After two naps, my mind felt energized. That is when I started thinking about my life and asking myself questions like:

What excites me about my current life? What kind of work is fulfilling to me? What would I like to change? How would I love my life to unfold? How do I want my marriage to be? What kind of a mom do I want to be? How do I want to spend my time on a typical day? What kind of impact do I want to make on the world? What makes me happiest? What are my least favorite things to do?

I want to point out that none of these questions were super specific, like how much money I wanted to make, how many kids I wanted, where I should travel, etc. I kept it very broad; more like the foundation of a house than the rooms and decor that go into the structure. I once read a book called *The Code of an Extraordinary Mind* by Vishen Lakhiani which goes into amazing detail about how to evaluate your life and what you want from it. If you struggle with the exercise I describe later in this chapter, grab that book. The author suggests that for each question you ask yourself, you need to get to the root or foundation of that answer. As an example, you may ask yourself What do I want out of life? Your answer could be I want to make a million dollars. From there, you need to keep going. Why do I want to make a million dollars? Your train of thought or follow-up questions may take you somewhere like this: I want to make a million dollars so that I can travel to cool places, see new things, and have flexibility in my work schedule, so that I have lots of time with my kids and can show them what other places in the world are like and that there are different cultures, so they are well-rounded individuals. Excuse the ridiculous run-on sentence, but that's like a stream of consciousness.

After this specific thought runs its course, you will have some core foundational values from it. You might say that adventure is important to you, as well as time with family and flexibility. Rather than just saying you want a million dollars, you now have more depth as to what you really want. The idea is to have a clear picture of how you want your life to be, so that as you shift through the different phases of life (from single to being in a relationship or from being in a relationship to being single, having children, changing career paths, moving to a new place, or losing family members), your life goals still make sense. If you say you want a million dollars, it may not always be relevant as you shift through life. More importantly, it doesn't connect with your emotions. But if you say you want adventure and flexibility, these ideals are more transferable and relevant no matter what happens in life. Adventure may look different when you're single than when you're married, right? But at the end of the day, you—whether single, married, or anything in between—value adventure. This is not to say that you will never change what you value or want to manifest in your life. You can certainly make changes as you develop and grow. Just make sure when you're making notes and getting clear on your life goals that you get to the root of each desire.

The idea is to have a clear picture of how you want your life to be so that as you shift through the different phases of life, your goals still make sense.

While I was alone for those 24 hours, after thinking about all these different life questions and journaling on them, I decided to drill down further on a couple of them. This is the step that many of us never take. We have a "vision" of what we want, but then never go any further. Why? It takes time. Not just regular time but *quiet* time. It may take 30 minutes or an hour or longer of just sitting quietly with no distractions, thinking. It takes time to get your mind off the day-to-day stuff and let it wander to a different place.

You want to let your mind go through the maze that it creates. Let your mind play out different scenarios. Give yourself time and space to evaluate how these different scenarios make you feel. Give yourself time and space to go through the ideas you first jotted down to cross some things out and add new ones. Be okay with some ideas that you felt so sure were important to you (like *really* important!) now being unimportant. This may be uncomfortable or boring at times. It may not feel like a productive use of time. This is exactly why some of us never fully complete this kind of exercise, but it's so worth it.

The only reason I completed it is because I literally had nothing else to do, nobody to talk to, and no technology to distract me for 24 hours.

You don't need to go to that extreme, but you certainly can if you want to. It was an epic 24 hours for me, I assure you. I felt energized, excited, and super focused. And I had all these epic notes in my journal that I can refer to forever when I need to remind myself of the experience. I also was really happy to connect with people after having solo time. If you can carve out even just one hour for yourself each week to work on this, within a month, you'll have an amazing foundation to move forward.

Here are some questions to ask yourself. As a starting point, think about the categories of health, finances, family, career, and spirituality. You can also print this worksheet at: https://tinyurl.com/GYSTchapter4 to write down your answers.

WHO DO I WANT TO BE?

1. What is great about my current life?

2. When am I happiest?

3. What gets me excited?

4. What kind of contribution do I want to make to the world?

5. What do I want to experience in life?

6. What is my ideal career?

7. Who is important in my life?

If you can't stand the thought of sitting still to do something like this, go for a walk. You can't listen to music or podcasts or an audiobook, though. Just walk. Start asking yourself some of the questions I noted above and see where your mind goes. Make sure when you're done walking, you *immediately* jot down notes. No matter how amazing your memory is, please write things down. Try to be detailed in your notes so you capture the emotion behind your thoughts. Sometimes, those emotions come and go so quickly that you'll never get them back without a little reminder for yourself. You can even take a notebook or a copy of the above worksheet with you on your walk and pause a couple of times to write. Whatever works for you. Just get your mind cranking. Let it go places it may not have gone since childhood when your mind was much freer.

Now that you've got this amazing vision for yourself and your life, you may experience some emotional backlash. The voices in your head may say *You'll never achieve your vision, you're not worthy of it, you're crazy to even think it.* Stop it! Just stop that right now. Thank those voices, which are really fear, for coming to say hello and for giving their input, and then kindly ask them to go away.

You *deserve* exactly what you want. *You are* worthy of anything and everything.

Chapter Summary

1. You need to know who you want to be, deep down in your core. This requires you to spend time alone, reflecting on your true values and desires. I promise, this is actually really fun!

2. Take the time to go through the exercise outlined in this chapter with the download I've provided or write on the worksheet in the book.

3. Keep this vision of who you want to be readily accessible. It should drive all decisions you make.

CHAPTER FIVE

Making Changes in Your Health

We're ready to dive into the how of getting your food, fitness, mindset, and overall well-being heading in the right direction. We all know what we are "supposed to" do: eat nutritious food, be active, get sleep, and drink plenty of water. So, what stops us? Is it that we have no willpower? Is it that we "can't" because of external influences (family, work, friends, etc.)?

You may say to yourself things like, *Maybe it's not what is intended for me; I'm just not cut out to have the kind of health I've always wanted.*

There is no truth in that statement. You haven't done the things you need to because of your mind, your thoughts, your emotions. How you think is the most powerful tool in your toolbox. How you think drives every action throughout the day.

The good news about this is that you have 100 percent control over these things. The bad news is that it requires daily effort to take back control after many years of letting your thoughts and emotions rule you.

Part I: Getting Started

Know Your Why   You need to get clear on the real purpose or drive behind making these changes. Changes aren't easy and generally speaking, they're not fun at first. So why would you commit to something hard, something that's clearly not fun? You'll only do it if you have a powerful underlying reason, maybe a pain point in your life that is unbearable. This is your *why*, and it needs to be front and center every single day. A quote by Darren Hardy, who I mentioned earlier as a highly successful entrepreneur and author, sums this concept up nicely.

> *Forget about willpower. It's time for why-power. Your choices are only meaningful when you connect them to your desires and dreams. The wisest and most motivating choices are the ones aligned with that which you identify as your purpose, your core self, and your highest values. You've got to want something and know why you want it, or you'll end up giving up too easily.*

My health "why" has always been that I like to feel strong and capable, and honestly, I like to feel good in my clothes. Additionally, I know that anytime I feel even slightly under the weather or I have something ailing me, it brings me down. It takes away from my happiness. Now that I have a daughter, I want to be healthy for as long as possible to be a part of her life. Doing anything I can to support my body functioning well is the daily goal.

Earlier, we talked about visualizing how you want your life to be, who you want to be, and what you place the most importance on in life. In that vision is your why. If you don't remember exactly what that vision was, revisit it now. Pull out your notes about what you want for yourself. Think specifically about your health and well-being and how that fits in with and serves your end goals. That's your why.

Identify Your Beliefs   A belief system is a set of principles guiding and governing a person's attitude. Another definition of belief systems I like: the stories we tell ourselves to define our personal sense of reality. I'm talking about subconscious beliefs, such as *Healthy food doesn't taste good*, that are part of your daily thoughts without you necessarily being aware of them. This example may not be true for you, but no matter who you are, you've got some deep-seated beliefs running your mind that I want you to be aware of.

Belief systems are formed in childhood, based on how we are raised and the narratives that we hear from parents, relatives, teachers, or any other influential people in our lives. Beliefs can come from seemingly innocent comments we hear often from those around us, like *Vegetables are rabbit food or There's no time for sleep when I've got mouths to feed*. We learn beliefs about food, money, sleep, relationships, authority, careers, marriage, status, and many other topics. Without awareness of the beliefs we learned as children—when we were little sponges absorbing ideas we didn't yet understand—these beliefs will carry on in us forever.

As adults, we have the choice to dig into our beliefs and decide for ourselves which ones we do believe and which ones we now find to be false. Those that we don't agree with and are not serving us can be changed. It's not an easy process, but it's 100 percent doable. You will find internal resistance as you consider changing certain beliefs; when you have lived under a certain set of principles for so long, it's going to feel strange at first to act in a new way. You may also find external resistance from your loved ones as you share your findings and express your thoughts about what you truly believe. Be prepared for this and know that it's okay. Identifying beliefs you acquired as a child and deciding that they're not right for you anymore doesn't mean that your parents/caregivers did anything wrong. There's no universal right or wrong. However, there is a right and a wrong for you in your own life. This is your chance to reflect on what you want out of life and mold your personal belief system to serve you in the best way possible.

Some common examples of beliefs around health and wellness are:

a) Healthy food is expensive
b) Healthy eating is complicated
c) Exercise is hard
d) I'm destined to be unhealthy because of my genetics
e) Fruits and vegetables aren't "real" foods
f) Getting a full night of sleep is a luxury
g) Focusing on my wellness is a luxury

Hopefully, this gives you an idea about what I mean by inner beliefs. And hopefully, at least one of these resonates with you. Spend a few minutes right now thinking about your beliefs when it comes to your health. There is a worksheet on the next page you can use to jot down what you come up with. There's also a printable version at https://tinyurl.com/GYSTbeliefsystems.

MY BELIEFS ABOUT HEALTH AND WELLI

Old Belief #1: _____

_____

_____

_____

New Belief #1: _____

_____

_____

_____

Old Belief #2: _____

_____

_____

_____

New Belief #2: _____

_____

_____

_____

Old Belief #3: _____

_____

_____

_____

New Belief #3: _____

_____

_____

_____

Now that you have a list, consider which ones you can start thinking differently about. Let's take the example of saying *healthy eating is complicated*. If this is a belief you hold, you have an immediate barrier in front of you when you're aiming to make healthier choices for your meals. You've got resistance before you even start. Now that you're aware of this belief, you can decide that you're going to start telling yourself a different story, maybe that *healthy eating is simple* or *healthy eating comes naturally to me*. Let go of the first belief and start telling yourself the new belief. Look for evidence that your new belief is true. This might be writing out a basic meal plan for one day so that you can see how simple it can be. This might be looking up a simple healthy recipe and watching a video on how to prepare it or doing a Google search to find a local restaurant you've never tried that offers healthier take-out options. Then, start living each day with a conscious effort to notice when old thinking comes up and replace it with your new thinking.

Changing your beliefs isn't an overnight process. With consistent work, you'll prove to yourself that your new set of beliefs is true and makes you feel good, and the shift will happen.

Be Intentional   Just like anything else in life, you need to have a plan and know your end goal. Similar to the visualization exercise we did in Chapter 4, if you don't know where you want to go, you're definitely not going to get there. Once you have that vision, you need more specific steps to follow. You don't need a full map, but you need some guidelines. For example, if you were planning a trip to a new city, you know exactly where you want to end up—likely your hotel—but you've got to make a few plans in between point A and point B to get there. Do you have to fly? Do you need ground transportation? You get the idea. So, when you say you're going to "eat better," that's fabulous, but what does that really mean? You need more definition in that end goal. Here are some examples of how to add structure to this goal. Work on:

a) Eating a vegetable with every meal
b) Eating five servings of fruits and vegetables per day
c) Drinking eight glasses of water a day
d) Getting eight hours of sleep each night
e) Meditating for five minutes a day

As you can see, this doesn't need to be anything really extreme, but you've got to have some kind of framework for daily focus. Choose one or two things to start with for the first couple of weeks, and then when those feel solid, reevaluate, and see if you're ready to add something else.

Short-term pain brings long-term happiness and health. Short-term pleasure will ultimately bring long-term pain.
—DARREN HARDY

Focus on the Long-Term   A slow and steady approach is far more sustainable than a quick but extreme method. Anything extreme probably isn't healthy for you anyway, physically or emotionally. I know you want results *now*. I totally get it! There are so many things in life that we can get now, like Amazon deliveries or Starbucks coffee. Those things are super cool, but that's not how the other areas of life work. To help get this long-term mindset in place, go back and look at your notes from Chapter 4 about what you want your life to look like. Remind yourself of the ultimate goal driving the changes you're making. I guarantee, none of the things you envision for yourself are short-term. Let's say you really want a loving relationship. Do you want that just for this month, or do you want that forever? Another example is if you envision yourself living to 100. That definitely isn't about short-term focus!

Do the Easy Stuff   If you blow off the easy stuff, you'll never reach your goals. What does this mean? Tiny decisions you make every day add up. They may seem inconsequential (one bite of this or that, skip one workout, stay up an hour later than you planned, etc.), but over time, they add up and absolutely impact your results. Get used to paying attention to the small, daily choices you make. They matter!

One thing you can do to help yourself get the easy stuff right is plan your schedule each week. I previously worked with a life coach who got me on a weekly planning routine and it made a dramatic, positive impact in my life.

When making a plan for the week, think about exercise, food, and sleep. Jot down your existing commitments like work, appointments, and extracurriculars. Then think about when you are going to exercise, when/where/what you will eat, and what time you need to go to bed to get a full night of sleep. Plan all these things out on paper or an electronic calendar. I like paper, as I can easily refer to it and make notes and check things off, even though I still have all important appointments and reminders on my electronic calendar. Once you have a plan, you can refer to it each day and make sure you follow through on your commitments. This can help you streamline grocery shopping, saving time and money. This also ensures you're not left with last minute indecision about what to eat, you won't get to the end of the week and realize you haven't exercised at all, and you won't have multiple nights in a row with insufficient sleep. Here's an example of what this might look like:

6:00 AM	Wake up
6:30 AM	Strength training workout
7:30 AM	Breakfast: Oatmeal and protein shake
8:30–noon	Work
Noon	Lunch: Salad with tofu
12:30–5 PM	Work
6:00 PM	Dinner: Chicken, roasted veggies, and quinoa
9:30 PM	Reading in bed
10:00 PM	Lights out

You can get as detailed as you like with this, but the basic things I want you to cover are exercise (see more details about the kind of exercise and frequency later in this chapter), meals, and sleep. If you know that you'll be eating out, put that on your calendar. If you like to have take-out sometimes, put that on your calendar and decide where you'll order from.

Get Support   I read an article about the number one differentiator personal trainers noted in whether or not someone was successful in meeting their goals: support. Whether an individual had good support or not made all the difference. This could be professional support, like a coach or trainer. This could be family and friends. The message is, don't try to do it solo. Don't keep it a secret. Ask for intentional support from your loved ones, even if that just means saying, *Hey, Friend. I'm setting some goals and they're really important to me. I need your help and support in succeeding.* If someone can't do that for you, keep asking until you find someone that can.

Here are some simple ways you can implement this:

a) Find a **mentor**, someone who has expertise or experience in whatever you're aiming to achieve. This might be a paid trainer, nutritionist, or coach. This might be an acquaintance or online personality who has "been there, done that." This can take on many different forms; there is no right or wrong way to work with a mentor as long as it works for both people and supports your goals.

b) Find an **accountability partner**, someone you trust to be real with you. This is different from a mentor because this person doesn't need to be experienced with your specific goal, they just need to be willing to be there for you. You can share what you're aiming to do with your accountability partner and check in with them once a week. It's important to have a scheduled check-in so that you know this person is going to want to hear how things are going. Maybe also have spontaneous check-ins as well, where you're able to reach out to this person in moments you need additional support or a little pep talk. If this person also has goals in mind, you can return the favor and be his/her accountability partner at the same time.

c) Find a **specific program or plan** that fits your goals; there are many wellness programs out there to choose from. Do some research and see if there's something that resonates with you. Consider your fitness, nutrition, and overall wellness goals, and of course, your budget. There are programs to fit any budget. If there isn't any built in accountability with the program you choose, combine this with my suggestion above and find someone to be your accountability partner. Better yet, find someone who will do it with you! But don't wait to start if you can't find a buddy. Just get moving and maybe you'll find a buddy along the way.

Quick Pep Talk About Self-Worth   When it comes to body image, I know from experience how much we can agonize over our bodies compared to other women's. It's mentally exhausting. If I could go back in time, I'd tell myself not to miss out on anything in life because I'm worried about what I look like in a bathing suit. My worth is not based on what my body looks like. Turning that statement around for you: *Your worth is not based on what your body looks like.* I support you 100 percent in working to be the healthiest version of yourself. That's what I want you to achieve. Let me be clear, though, that this isn't tied in with your worth or your character. Working toward achieving health and well-being is about feeling confident, physically and mentally strong, happy, and capable. It's not about becoming a good person or getting yourself to a position where you are now worthy of some article of clothing, love from someone, or being treated kindly. Wherever you are right now in life, *you're already enough.* You're already worthy of love, happiness, and anything your heart desires.

If you're someone that feels a lot of hate toward your body, know that I have been in your shoes. I'm reaching out right now to give you a huge hug. When I was at my heaviest, I recall looking at other women on my college campus and wanting so badly to be thinner. It was a terrible feeling. Day by day, as I made positive changes in my life, I felt more confident. Little by little, over the years, this shifted. I still have some of those same insecurities pop up now; after all, I am human. But I've got tools and life experience to help me handle them.

While working on your goals, it's really important not to hide from yourself. Even if you're tempted, don't cover up your body all the time. Take a minute every day, maybe after you shower, to look at your body; really look at it and take it in. When you hide your body from your own view, it perpetuates the hate. Our imaginations are far worse than reality, so stay connected with your real-life body. Remember that your body does incredible things for you every darn day. Give it a little love.

Part II: The How-To of Nutrition

Before we dive into this section, I want to define for you what I mean when I talk about *healthy* eating. When I use the word healthy when referring to foods, I mean foods that have a lot of nutrients. It's that simple. There are no good or bad foods, just foods that either have a lot of nutrients or don't.

How Should You Be Eating?   You can make any specific way of eating work for you as long as it's based on eating real food. If you feel good eating a lower carbohydrate diet, like a paleo-style diet, or a balance of all macronutrients (proteins, carbohydrates, and fat), go for it. If you want to eat a vegetarian or vegan diet, do it! Or, if you feel like eating based on listening to your body and what it needs in any given moment, more of an intuitive eating approach, go for that, although it may be tougher for some people, depending on their previous eating habits, but it's not impossible. I've listened to many nutritionists, dietitians, and doctors talk about how to eat, and there are compelling arguments made for any style of eating out there. Because of expert research on so many different ways of eating, I will never say that the way I eat is the way everyone should eat. Each person is different and needs to find what makes them feel good—following one basic principle.

The main focus should be on eating real, Mo,
foods. Fruits, vegetables, whole grains, legumes,
quality protein. Reflecting on the experts I've learnec
years, the one commonality among all of their advice is ,
foods over processed foods. Can you get all the **macro**nutri,
ros") you need from eating processed foods? Yes. Can you ,
micronutrients (vitamins, minerals, and phytonutrients) yc ,ced
from eating processed foods? The food manufacturers may argue yes,
but I say no. You can buy processed foods that are fortified with
micronutrients, but it's not the same as eating whole foods naturally
providing those same nutrients.

I recently picked up the book *Superlife* by Darin Olien, who is
touted as the "superfood hunter." He has traveled around the world for
many years learning about foods that have helped sustain different
groups of people. What Olien shares about nutrition in his book is different from anything I've ever read about nutrition. He shares the
results of global studies on how whole foods versus processed foods
impact our bodies. Without giving away too much, I will say that my
stand on the importance of whole, plant-based foods became even
stronger after reading his book. Scientists can't possibly know all the
changes that occur in a food when you break it down from its natural
form (a.k.a. processing it into something else). What they do know is
that the body processes and digests whole foods more effectively.
Superlife talks about a study at Pomona College published in *Food &*
Nutrition Research where two groups of individuals were given meals
with identical calories and macronutrients (fat, carbohydrates, and
proteins), but one group ate whole foods and the other group ate all
processed, packaged foods. The group eating only processed foods
burned half as many calories as the group eating whole foods. The

authors of the study concluded that the consumption of processed foods results in "increased energy assimilation and may be a contributor to weight gain." To me, this means our bodies don't know how to use processed foods in the same way that they do whole foods. This makes sense! Foods grown naturally is what Mother Earth intended us to eat.

The difference in cost between processed foods and whole foods can be a barrier—it's silly how cheap some packaged foods are. That should tell you, though, how low quality the ingredients in those foods are. Every food manufacturer prices their products so that they make a profit. Therefore, if the end price is low, you can work backward to get an idea as to what it costs the manufacturer to produce that product, and the number of people they expect to buy it. When money is tight and you are trying to feed a whole family, I understand that you need to do your best with your budget, but consider the cost of your food decisions today on your health down the road. To quote *Superlife*: "Would we rather give our money to the farmer or the pharmacist, the grocer or the doctor?" Spending a little extra on your food now and throughout your life should save you on healthcare costs later.

The earth we live on is pretty darn spectacular. If you think about all the cycles of life on this planet, how each species is designed to survive, it's phenomenal. Every species, other than humans, feeds off what the earth creates. We humans have a different mental capacity and come up with our own version of food. On the one hand, our mental capacity is extraordinary in what it can do. On the other hand, it is not serving us in positive ways when it comes to food. Why do we think we're smarter than the earth? We're not. We don't even understand all the intricacies of nature. We're fighting so darn hard against nature that we're literally killing ourselves and leaving in our wake nasty consequences for the rest of the planet by way of plastic, trash, and pollutants. How clever would someone think our species is if they were watching from a distance? They would think we are nuts for destroying ourselves and that we're jerks for taking other parts of nature down with us.

We've gotten so far away from what earth intended we eat. While we are never going back to living off the land 100 percent again, given our current circumstances—surrounded by thousands of processed food choices—we have to individually decide for ourselves that the best choices are whole foods. Our bodies were created to eat whole foods, so if we want them to function at an optimal level and avoid disease, we've got to feed them whole foods. End of story.

As you start eating healthier foods consistently, you'll feel the benefits outweigh your emotional desire for a burger and fries. More importantly, as healthy foods become a staple in your diet, the donuts and pizza won't even appeal to you anymore. Your taste buds change. You may be rolling your eyes ... that's okay; I see it from my husband often. I've been there too, craving burritos and ice cream every day. These foods are addictive and are designed that way! Their producers want you to buy more. They are not concerned with the impact these foods have on your health, but rather, the profitability of their brands.

I've also been one to crave vegetables, salads, and just overall fresh foods. This is way better. I still enjoy pizza, nachos, fries, and sweets when I really want them. But, feeling mentally clear, having healthy digestion and normal blood sugar levels, fitting easily into my clothes, and being strong make me much happier than eating junk food on a regular basis.

Based on a discussion with a good friend about weight loss and food addiction, I include a caveat here that there *are* circumstances, whether medical or mental health related, that can inhibit your ability, or lack thereof, to change the habits we're discussing. If you know you are dealing with such circumstances, I recommend working with a professional. This may be a doctor, nutritionist, or mental health professional.

I know many people like specific examples, so I've provided a couple of sample meal plans for you at the end of this section. These plans are just examples; if you don't like one of the food items you see, swap it out for another healthy food. Overall, though, don't get too wrapped up in planning a perfect meal. Aim to include fruits, vegetables, grains or other complex carbohydrates, healthy fats, and protein in your diet each day.

Please note that these meal plans are roughly what I would eat in a day and I'm a 125-pound female who exercises 30–60 minutes, five days a week. I also move a lot throughout the day, going for walks and not sitting idle for too long except to work. If your level of activity differs from this, you will need to adjust the amount you eat. How much? Well ... eat until you're full, and not more than that. But don't leave yourself hungry. If you're hungry, eat!

Hunger   Following a healthy diet is not about deprivation. However, you also need to check in with yourself if you *think* you're hungry. Take a moment to focus on what the supposed hunger is all about. If it truly is nutritional hunger, please eat more! If the hunger is more emotional, pause for a moment and see if there's something else going on that you can resolve in a different way. Let me give you a couple of examples of what I mean.

Let's say you're at work and having a stressful day. Your boss has been breathing down your neck about a project that needs to be completed and you're doing your best, but it doesn't feel like enough. You take a short bathroom break and, on your way back to your desk you swing by the office snack cupboard. (Doesn't every office have one of those now?) You're there staring at the options, deciding what to choose. Pretzels, chocolate-covered almonds, chips, or an apple. Before you even think about the best option for yourself in this situation, I want you to stop and consider if you're actually hungry. Are you physically hungry or are you looking for a quick shot of happiness to soothe your emotional state? Only you can know if it's the former or latter. If you come to the conclusion that this is more of an emotional hunger, try another solution like taking a quick walk around the block or stopping to chat with a coworker who you know will cheer you up.

Here's another example. This one really hits home for me, and I know I'm not alone. You're at home, enjoying your favorite TV show after a delicious and satisfying dinner. A little itch starts in your belly (or your mind) and you think a post-dinner snack is in order. You contemplate it for 15 minutes and eventually get up and go to the pantry. Opening the door, your eyes are searching to see what looks good. I'll stop here because we all know how this plays out. In this exact moment, I encourage you to ask yourself if you're really hungry. Maybe you are, but maybe you are feeling tired or lonely and want a little pick-me-up. My number one suggestion here is to go to bed. We are often short on sleep and we fight so hard to stay up just a little later than we need to. Turn the TV off, brush your teeth, slip into your pajamas and get in that super comfy bed. If it's just too darn early for bed (which for me, there's no such thing, but I realize not everyone is like that—I'm married to one of those people), call a friend and make a connection. Get your "fix" through a fun conversation. You're probably doing that friend a favor too—maybe he or she really needed some human connection as well. Another thing you can do is grab that book or magazine lying around the house that you've been wanting to read. Get some mental stimulation going. I'm in this situation far more often since my daughter was born; being "stuck" at home with my little one and having the craziest hunger pangs I've ever experienced. Sometimes, I go for the evening snacks and sometimes I don't. Neither one is good or bad. The point is to be aware of these moments and learn from them.

Overall, what I'm asking you to do is check in with yourself regarding your "hunger." Hunger isn't bad. Neither is snacking. I snack often. But, there are different kinds of hunger, including hunger for hydration (drink that H_2O), so learning to decipher the needs your body is signaling is super helpful in managing your food intake. It's also helpful in learning about yourself and finding outlets for emotions other than food.

Portion Size   If you're new to the concept of watching portion sizes, it will take some experimentation. As you do, it's important to eat slowly. I'm not always good at this myself, trust me. But eating slowly allows your stomach to feel full as you're eating. If you don't have time to slow down for whatever reason, then at least give yourself 15–20 minutes after you've finished eating before deciding whether you really need more. There are times I don't do this because I feel some sort of urgency that I can only eat now or never, and it often leaves me fuller than I really want to be.

If you haven't ever paid attention to portions, tracking what you eat in some kind of app or on paper can be helpful. The purpose is not to become obsessed with what you're eating and how much, but to bring awareness about how you eat; like whether you tend to eat more at a specific meal, and how often you eat. You may learn that you need a big breakfast (like me), so you can plan for that. You may learn that you tend to snack a lot between lunch and dinner, so consider changing meal times or eating more at lunch if that's helpful for you.

If you choose to track your food, do it for a couple of weeks just to gauge your habits, then you don't need to do it any further. From my experience, tracking every bite you take for any length of time can be damaging to your emotional well-being and ultimately cause you to eat more.

As you build knowledge around what your body really needs, you'll notice that your hunger levels aren't static. Based on activity levels, hormonal cycles, stress, or other factors, you'll need more food on certain days and less on others. This is why I can't get behind any specific, defined meal plan that works for everyone. We are individuals. I know many of us want someone to just tell us **exactly** what to eat and how much, but you need to experiment—with whole foods, not processed stuff—for yourself, and I promise you'll find a groove.

A beautiful way to wrap this section up is by letting you know that once you start eating more and more whole foods, some of the cravings you may be used to will literally disappear. When your body is nutritionally satisfied from the food you're consuming, salt, fat, and sugar cravings diminish. Then, when your body is balanced with the right nutrients, you'll notice that if a craving does come up, it means that there really is something your body needs.

As you transition away from processed foods, you may encounter a period when the unprocessed foods don't taste as good as the processed foods you're used to. There's no avoiding this if your taste buds are used to tons of oils, salt, and sugar! As I've said, change isn't easy or fun. It can really suck sometimes. But your taste buds will adjust as you continue eating whole foods. And then your taste buds will **love** the natural sweetness you get from watermelon, the delicious flavor of avocados, and the divine nuttiness from fresh cooked barley. Your body will start to recognize these flavors and know exactly what to do with the foods you're consuming, using the nutrients it needs and getting rid of the rest. You'll grow to love the flavors of fresh salad ingredients mixed together and roasted vegetables ... even if you're a self-proclaimed vegetable hater. I promise!

Sample Menus   I've included a couple of sample menus. Remember, these are written for my weight and activity level. You need to modify quantities to fit your current weight and activity level. If there are foods here that you hate, swap them out for something you love. But I also encourage you to get adventurous with new foods. Try fruits, vegetables, or grains that you've never tried before. And prepare them in different ways. There are so many different foods, maybe you'll stumble across something that you just can't live without. The more varieties of plant foods you regularly incorporate into your diet, rather than just the same 5–10 fruits and vegetables, the better it is for your body.

Also, make a concerted effort to actually **taste** the food you're eating. You may find that when you do, you truly enjoy foods you previously disliked, and maybe you don't love the taste of other foods that previously made your heart skip a beat. Foods can be associated with memories. Foods can trigger emotions. It's possible you're placing some foods on a pedestal and others in the gutter based on memories or emotions, rather than actual taste.

In any meal plan, include plenty of water. A good rule of thumb is to take your weight and halve that. That's your goal for ounces of water per day; if you're 150 pounds, aim for 75 ounces of water. If you're 200 pounds, aim for 100 ounces of water. This is really important to your overall nutrition. Don't skip it, and please track it for a couple of days to know how you're doing.

Vegan Menu (roughly 45% carbs/35% fat/20% prot
Breakfast:
- —Smoothie with 1 serving of plant-based protein po
  spinach, ½ cup blueberries, 1 tbsp. ground flaxsee
  water (or milk of choice), ice
- —½ cup plain oatmeal, ½ tbsp nut butter, sprinkle of u
  shreds or cacao nibs

Snack:
- —1 cup sliced carrots and celery with ¼ cup hummus

Lunch:
- —Mixed green salad with ½ cucumber, ¼ avocado, ½ block of tempeh, 1
  tbsp pumpkin seeds, and balsamic vinaigrette

Snack:
- —Apple and ¼ cup of mixed nuts/seeds (preferably raw)

Dinner:
- —Baked sweet potato, sliced in half, topped with ½ cup black beans and
  salsa, and a side of sautéed kale

Balanced Macro Menu (roughly 40% carbs/30% fat/30% protein):
Breakfast:
- —Smoothie with 1 serving of plant-based protein powder, ½ cup frozen
  spinach, ½ cup blueberries, 1 tbsp ground flaxseed, pinch of cinnamon,
  water (or milk of choice), ice
- —½ cup plain oatmeal, ½ tbsp nut butter, sprinkle of unsweetened coconut
  shreds or cacao nibs

Snack:
- —1 cup sliced zucchini with ¼ cup hummus

Lunch:
- —Mixed green salad with ½ cucumber, ¼ avocado, 1 chicken breast,
  1 tbsp pumpkin seeds, and balsamic vinaigrette
- —½ cup quinoa or ½ whole wheat pita bread

Snack:
- —Apple and ½ cup plain Greek yogurt with pinch of cinnamon, plus a half
  dozen or so raw almonds

Dinner:
- —3–4ozs Grilled salmon, ½ sweet potato, and sautéed kale

Menu (higher protein, lower carb):
Breakfast:
—2 eggs, 2 slices turkey bacon, sautéed spinach
Snack:
—1 cup celery sticks and cucumber with ¼ cup almond butter
Lunch:
—1 chicken breast, 2 cups roasted broccoli and cauliflower, ¼ avocado
 with a sprinkle of hemp seeds
Snack:
—Apple
Dinner:
—Shrimp stir-fry with kale, peppers, and bok choy with sesame seeds

You'll notice that these meals are pretty basic. Food should be simple. If you're an amazing chef, get wild with your meals. For many of us, that's not easy and deters us from making our own food. If these meals feel too simple, spice them up however you like with other real foods or stick with simple meals most days but plan for a couple of times a week to get more creative and fun with your food when you have time. If you're not usually a salad eater, do me a favor and try to eat one a few times a week. Salads are one of the quickest meals to throw together if you have the ingredients on hand. You can make them delicious and satisfying by adding more than just lettuce and tomatoes. Throw in avocado, sweet potato, beets, walnuts, shredded carrots and zucchini, beans, apples, seeds, chicken, salmon, or anything that sounds good to you. I added a few recipes at the end of this section, including a great salad recipe, so you have a place to start.

Some of my favorite food choices are listed below, bearing in mind that I'm a primarily plant-based eater, with occasional fish, eggs, and dairy. As I've said, any style of eating can work if you apply it consistently and stick with unprocessed foods. However, to give your body optimal health (which means healthy insides not just a sexy outside), protein shouldn't be as big of a focus as the nutrition industry has led us to believe. Protein is essential, but you can get protein from all kinds of food, not just large servings of animal meat. Nuts, seeds, vegetables, legumes, and grains all have protein. If you incorporate these foods into your diet regularly, you'll get plenty of protein. If you want to then add some small portions of specific "protein foods" like salmon, chicken, turkey, tofu, or yogurt, do it. Aim to keep your plate no more than 25 percent protein. The rest of your plate should be filled with vegetables and whole grains or legumes.

Reading Labels

As we're on the subject of grocery shopping, it's important that I talk briefly about reading labels on food products. This may be something you already do and feel confident with. If so, great. If not, here's why you need to start doing it. All packaged foods are required to have labels outlining the nutrition information: calories, total fat, saturated fat, sugar, protein, sodium, carbohydrates, cholesterol, and other nutrients. They also have to list ingredients. It's a lot of information to take in, but it can be very helpful when choosing what to buy. I like to focus on a couple of things when I look at a label.

I tend to look for a few things immediately when checking an **ingredient list**. How long is the list? Usually, a shorter list of ingredients is best. This isn't always the case, as some products have a lot of different vegetables or herbs/spices added, but typically, a short list is a good thing. Next, I look at the actual ingredients. Do I recognize what's in this product? If the words aren't familiar to me, that's a bad sign as that means artificial ingredients and preservatives have been added. Finally, I consider which ingredients are listed first. The ingredients should be listed in order of quantity, from greatest to least, meaning the first ingredient(s) make up the bulk of the finished product. If the first or second ingredient listed is sugar, some kind of fat, or something you don't recognize, I'd put that down and move on.

When I look at the **nutrition facts** (calories, fat, etc.), I look first at the serving size. Every label should tell you what the manufacturer considers one serving of the product; that is what they are basing their numbers on. As an example, if you pick up a bag of chips, the label may say that one serving is 10 chips and that there are 10 servings per bag. Now you know that as you read further down the label and see that there are 150 calories and 8 grams of fat, those values are referring to one serving, or 10 chips. Therefore, the entire bag of chips, which is 10 servings, is 10 times the amount listed on the label. Some products do show both single and full product serving nutrition information, but most do not. This is so important as serving sizes can vary wildly from brand to brand and are sometimes unrealistically small. You'll notice that sometimes even a food that you think is just one serving, like a small bag of chips or a candy bar, isn't treated as a single serving by the manufacturer when it comes to the label. You pick up the candy bar and see initially it says 150 calories and 10g sugar and think, *that's not so bad*. You then see there are two servings, so if you eat the whole thing that's really 300 calories and 20g sugar. You may feel differently about that purchase after fully understanding the servings.

Next, I look at **sugars**. If the label lists total sugars as well as added sugars, the added sugars is what I'm most interested in. There may be sugar in a product because it has fruit, which I'm comfortable with. But if there's a lot of *added* sugar, I'm not comfortable with that, or I at least want to be aware of that! As you read more labels, you'll be surprised how many things have added sugar. Even savory food items like bread, pasta sauce, and crackers can have a lot of added sugar. Flavored yogurts and cereals are also ones to pay close attention to. If you like flavored coffee drinks, check out the nutrition information for those. All of the major coffee chains provide nutrition information for their drinks and food items on their websites. You may be getting 15g or more of added sugar from your morning pick-me-up (even just a basic latte if there's sweetened milk), so it's good to know what you're putting in your body.

Finally, I like to look at **saturated fats and sodium**. Packaged foods can contain copious amounts of both. Sodium, in particular, can get out of control if you're consuming a lot of packaged foods. Saturated fat isn't always a bad thing, depending on the source and what else you're consuming on a daily basis, but it's something to be aware of.

I could go on a lot more in terms of label reading, but this is a good foundation to start with. If this is new to you, take it one step at a time. Take your time looking at the labels of products you already have in your cupboard. Look at the ingredients, serving size, sugars, and the other numbers you find. See what you learn. Once you understand how labels are organized, you can quickly check them while shopping so that you're not spending hours at the store. Also, once you get to know which brands you trust in terms of quality ingredients, you don't even have to look at the labels. Keep in mind that the more unpackaged foods you buy, like fresh produce, the fewer labels you have to look at!

Recipes

At the suggestion of my husband, who is a great cook, I'm including a few recipes that are easy enough for anybody to execute (even novices like me), but also give you a meal that feels a little fancier than a basic plate filled with a protein, a vegetable, and a complex carbohydrate. I consulted with him to make sure the final product had his stamp of approval. You can also download the recipes at https://tinyurl.com /GYSTrecipes.

Hearty Wholesome Salad

Makes 2 servings

- —2 cups spinach
- —2 cups loose leaf lettuce (red or green)
- —1 cucumber, sliced and quartered
- —½ cup shredded zucchini
- —½ cup shredded carrot
- —½ avocado, sliced
- —¼ cup sunflower seeds
- —1 grilled chicken breast or 8 oz. grilled tofu (optional)
- —1 tbsp extra virgin olive oil
- —1 tbsp balsamic vinegar
- —Pinch of sea salt
- —Pinch of ground black pepper
- —Pinch of garlic powder

Instructions:

1. In a large bowl, add spinach, lettuce, cucumber, zucchini, carrot, and sunflower seeds. The avocado will be added later. Using tongs, mix the ingredients together.
2. To make the dressing, combine olive oil, balsamic vinegar, salt, black pepper, and garlic powder in a mason jar or other container that can be sealed. Close the container and give it a few shakes. Adjust seasonings to taste.
3. Pour dressing evenly over salad and use the tongs to toss the salad a few times.
4. Divide the salad into two serving bowls and add ¼ of the sliced avocado and ½ of the protein (chicken or tofu) to each.

Other notes: This recipe is summer-y so if you want something for cooler weather, you can swap out the lettuces for kale. With raw kale, I recommend chopping it and massaging it with your hands in a bowl with a little olive oil for a few minutes before it goes into your salad. You can also remove the cucumber, zucchini, and carrots and add in cubes of roasted sweet potato and roasted brussels sprouts. Other modifications can be different kinds of seeds, like pumpkin, or dried cranberries. Throw in ½ cup of cooked quinoa, barley, or farro to make this even more filling. And don't forget about beans! Throw in a cup of white beans, especially if you're not adding chicken or tofu. All of these ingredients are available at major grocery stores and many of them can be found at discount grocery stores too. All of the dressing ingredients are good ones to look for at discount stores.

Cauliflower Tacos

Makes 2 servings

- —4 corn tortillas
- —2 cups cauliflower florets
- —1 tbsp olive oil
- —1 tsp salt
- —½ tsp cumin
- —½ tsp coriander
- —½ tsp chili powder
- —½ tsp garlic powder
- —½ tsp pepper
- —¼ tsp cayenne
- —1 can organic black beans
- —1 tbsp tahini
- —½ tbsp lime juice (the juice of one lime)
- —¼ cup shredded Cheddar cheese (optional)
- —Avocado (optional)
- —Mango salsa (optional)

Instructions:

1. Mix all of the dry spices together. Set 1 tsp of the mixture aside. Toss the cauliflower florets with the olive oil and then with 1 tsp of spice mixture.
2. Mix the tahini, lime juice, and ½ tsp of spice mixture together in a small container.
3. Drain three-quarters of the liquid from the beans and place in a pot. Add ½ cup of water and cook them on medium-high heat. While they are cooking, mash the beans with a fork until you have a spreadable paste.
4. Roast the cauliflower florets at 400°F for 10 minutes. They should be slightly firm and slightly caramelized.
5. Warm the tortillas.
6. Spread the bean paste onto one side of the tortilla, top with cauliflower, and drizzle with the tahini-lime mixture. Then top with cheddar cheese, avocado, and/or mango salsa. Shredded cabbage and a hot sauce of your choice can be added as well, but the base of this delicious taco is tortilla, black bean paste, roasted cauliflower, and the tahini-lime drizzle.

Baked Herb Garlic Salmon in Foil, with Vegetables

Makes 2 servings

- —½ lb. salmon
- —2 cups chopped broccoli
- —½ cup uncooked quinoa (any color)
- —2 tbsp extra virgin olive oil (optional)
- —¼ teaspoon dill or parsley
- —¼ teaspoon garlic powder
- —¼ teaspoon onion powder
- —¼ teaspoon sea salt
- —¼ teaspoon black pepper
- —1 lemon, halved

Instructions:

1. Preheat oven to 400°F.
2. In a medium pot, add ¾ cup water, quinoa (rinsed in a colander), and a dash of salt.
3. Bring water to a boil and then cover and cook over low heat until tender, about 15 minutes.
4. While quinoa is cooking, line a baking sheet with a piece of aluminum foil.
5. In a small bowl, mix all seasonings together.
6. Place the salmon in the center of the aluminum foil and rub with 1 tbsp olive oil (this is optional because salmon already is a fatty fish and I don't feel the need for olive oil, but chefs would likely disagree, even if just to get the herbs to stay in place).
7. Sprinkle the herb seasoning on the salmon.
8. Squeeze juice from ½ lemon on the salmon.
9. Fold the foil on the salmon, ensuring all sides are closed.
10. On the same baking sheet, place your chopped broccoli around the salmon. Drizzle 1 tbsp of olive oil over the top and add a dash of sea salt and black pepper to taste.
11. Put the baking sheet in the oven and cook 10–15 minutes.

Antioxidant-Rich Berry Nutty Oats

Makes 2 servings
- −1 cup rolled oats
- −1 cup blueberries (frozen or fresh)
- −1 tbsp almond butter (preferably unsalted)
- −2 tsp ground flaxseed
- −¼ tsp ground cinnamon
- −1 tbsp chopped walnuts

Instructions:

1. Place oats, almond butter, flaxseed, and cinnamon together in a bowl.
2. Pour boiling water over the oats mixture and stir so ingredients mix together and are moistened.
3. Cover bowl and let it sit 3–4 minutes.
4. Divide the mixture between two bowls, then sprinkle ½ of the blueberries and ½ of the walnuts into each bowl.

You can do many different variations on this dish by changing up the fruit, the nuts, the spices, or even the grain (quinoa is delicious). You can also add a protein powder to the mixture, use dairy or soy milk in lieu of water, or top it with a dollop of plain Greek yogurt to give it more protein. If you substitute milk for water, you can warm the milk first and add to the oats mixture, or add cold milk, then heat it in the microwave or in a pot on the stove. You can also add an egg on the side if you want a larger meal.

Part III: The How-To for Exercise

I'm not going to spend a lot of time on the "how-to" of physical exercise, but I can't exclude it from our discussion. Exercise is very important for your overall health and well-being. Fitness is one of my favorite parts of healthy living! I truly love working out and doing different types of exercise. Do I always love the thought of it beforehand? Heck, no! Do I love the feeling I have after a workout is complete? Heck, yes! Feeling out of breath and sweaty gives me the best high in life; better than any alcohol buzz I've ever had. There's a saying, "The only workout you regret is the one you didn't do" and I'm a believer. I can't remember a time when I worked out or moved my body and later felt I could've spent my time better in another way.

Physical Exercise and Your Overall Health   While exercise isn't the main driver of weight loss (focus on your food first), it's beneficial for your body and overall health in so many ways. If you look at the human body and how it works, you can see we are built for action. We have incredible physical strength, agility, and capacity for movement. If you need a reminder of this, look at the flexibility of babies and the way kids play. They don't stop when they start to get out of breath or sweat beads up on their faces. They keep moving until the point of exhaustion—literally—and with huge smiles on their faces! At what age does this stop and why? Maybe it's as we get older and "cooler," or when we become aware of how we look and don't want to get dirty or sweaty. I have moments, following my 14-month-old daughter around, that I think surely she needs a break from moving, from being in a squat position while she's sorting rocks, or from walking back and forth between trees. But that's never the case. Sure, I realize that as we grow up, we do get taller and heavier and further away from the ground so things like squatting become harder, but that doesn't mean we should stop moving or doing things that tire us out.

Before modern society, before fancy workout classes existed, before treadmills and dumbbells were invented, we had no choice but to be active. Whether we were walking to gather food, hunting down animals, fighting off threats to our families, building shelter, or using our physical strength to prepare food (think about grinding grains with a pestle and mortar), we had to be active to survive. There were no comfy couches for us to melt into with Netflix, no Uber Eats to bring us whatever we craved, no cars to take us to any store or coffee drive-through we wanted. In modern times, we literally have no need to do anything physical except get out of bed, brush our teeth, shower, and take a few steps between our house and the car and then back inside again. Get the picture?

We've created a very "easy" life for ourselves if we choose it. We are now in a situation where we need to create opportunities for exercise in our lives. Take a walk. Do some housework. Pull weeds. If you don't have a yard, pull weeds at a local park; I'm sure nobody will mind the help! There's a concept called NEAT, which stands for Non-Exercise Activity Thermogenesis. This describes the calories burned from normal day-to-day activities rather than structured exercise. This can include calories burned while walking around the grocery store, cooking, vacuuming, dancing to a great song that comes on, or carrying groceries from your car to your kitchen. These movements in our lives can have a huge positive impact on our health in terms of mood, calories burned, and improving other normal functions of the body. If you think about a scheduled exercise session that is 30 minutes, that's roughly 2 percent of your day. The rest of your awake time (more than 60 percent) gives you so much more time to get some movement in without even thinking about it. Even if you skip the structured workout altogether and just DO life in an active way, you'll burn calories and feel great. But this means you need to intentionally "do" some things. You've got to get off the couch and move.

Here is a short list of my favorite benefits of exercise:

1. Physical strength—Building muscle supports your skeletal structure and helps to prevent injury. It also burns more calories.

2. Mental strength—Exercising is great for your mind. It encourages deep thinking, builds confidence, and helps sharpen your focus. By proving to yourself that you can do hard things physically, you're building that mental muscle that gives you the confidence that you can do other hard things that come your way.

3. The aftermath effect—By doing some kind of physical exercise, you get yourself in a better mindset so that the rest of your awake time ends up being healthier, a.k.a. the "aftermath" effect. After a workout, you're more likely to choose nutrient-dense foods and be in a positive mental space.

4. Supporting all other physiological processes in our bodies—Exercising facilitates many processes we're not even aware of, like digestion and oxygenation. To truly close the full loop of what our bodies do internally, exercise is a must.

If you're not already into fitness, start by trying different types of exercise. Maybe even start with going for daily walks. When I lived overseas and began walking just to get to the train station, then to my office, and back home at night, I dropped a few pounds without even trying. I also had the chance to be outdoors, have some quiet "me"

time, and listen to great music or podcasts. \
able during my pregnancy, both physically an

Walking is discussed in *The Blue Zones*
book takes the reader to all the Blue Zone\
where a high percentage of centenarians live.
ities between these people was moderate exerc
people doing cross-fit or extreme forms of exe
viduals did a lot of walking or low-impact but p ... .ngs like
gardening.

There are many fitness options. You've got options you can do for
zero to minimal cost: walking, jogging, home-based weight training,
dancing, yoga, intramural sports, etc. It doesn't need to be anything
fancy or structured. Maybe it only works for you to squeeze in a couple
of 10-minute sessions during your day. Squats, push-ups, crunches,
lunges, and jumping jacks are all things you can do anywhere, anytime, and you don't even need to wear special workout clothes.

You've also got options if you want to spend money: gym mem-
berships, a personal trainer, cross-fit, private studios for yoga/Pilates/
barre/dance, home-based subscriptions like Beachbody on Demand
or Peloton.

Find something that you enjoy, or at least don't hate; something
that makes you feel great each time you finish the activity. Make sure
it challenges you! If you're not getting your heart rate up, not feeling a little sweat coming on, and not feeling out of breath, put more
effort into whatever you're doing. Yes, you can and should feel all of
those things with any form of exercise, even yoga or walking. And
don't give up on yourself. If exercise is new to you, you're going to get
tired, you're going to feel sore, and you may notice an increase in your
appetite. These things are all okay. If you need to eat more, do it. If

re, do some extra stretching or take a warm bath. But don't
at stop you from continuing the activity the next day. You are
stronger than you think.

Also, give some thought to what you truly want out of exercise.
This can help you decide what will serve you best in reaching your
goals. Do you want to gain muscle tone? Do you want to experience
high-intensity exercises? Do you want to work on flexibility? Do you
want to be outdoors? Do you want to be with other people? Do you
want to be able to have music or a podcast on while you're exercising?
These are all good questions to ask yourself. Then narrow down your
options and pick something.

How often to exercise is up to you and your schedule, but I say
three days a week should be your minimum. Assuming you stag-
ger your workouts to every other day, you'll never go more than two
days without a workout. Why does that matter? It keeps the habit in
place! If you go three or four days without any form of exercise, it
becomes easier to keep putting it off until "tomorrow." Make a commitment to yourself about how often you'll exercise and schedule
that on your calendar. Literally write it or type in into your calendar.
I can't emphasize that enough. Give your exercise commitment the
same importance as a business meeting or other appointment. This
not only makes the vow stronger in your mind, but it forces you to
think about when exercise will actually work in your schedule. You
can't possibly double-book yourself if you're looking at your calendar
and writing this down.

Set yourself up for success by getting yourself ready for your
exercise session. If you decide on a morning time slot for your fitness,
make sure you're ready to go the night before with your alarm set,
clothes out and ready to go, and the coffee queued up to brew if you
need that to start your day. Since I work out at home, solo and very

early, I sometimes wear part of my exercise clothes to bed the night before so that getting dressed in the morning is just a tiny bit quicker.

If you are going to exercise during your workday, get your fitness bag packed the night before. If you're joining a fitness class, make sure you've already booked your place ahead of time. If you have made a commitment to do something and you're waiting until the last second to book your spot in a class, I'm going to call you out and say you aren't fully committed. Don't leave any room to back out at the last minute. Excuses will come up in your head every single day; *I need more sleep, I really need to catch up on emails, my friend invited me for a glass of wine, a new project landed on my desk,* or even the excuse *I'm sore!* may arise on a daily basis. Don't let those things get you sidetracked. Once in a while, true emergencies do come up and you've got to shift your schedule around. That's just life. But if you get the exercise habit in place by following through on your commitment to yourself 95 percent of the time, you'll be setting yourself up for success. Remember when I talked about the beautiful situation you can get yourself in, where your habits are so ingrained that you don't even have to think about them anymore? That any "decision" about whether to exercise or not each day goes away? That is what I'm talking about here. And each day that you do what you promised yourself you'd do, your confidence grows. You build up that mental strength muscle.

To sum it up, getting some daily movement in your schedule is important for your body and your mind, but it doesn't need to be triathlon training. I've discussed exercise with many people, and sometimes the very first barrier is thinking that he or she can't do the things they see other people doing on Instagram, YouTube, or even around their neighborhood. You don't need to do those things. Start with walking, low-impact cardio workouts, or strength training with light weights (one to five pounds) or even with no weights. Go at your own pace and find something that fits your personality and lifestyle. Stick with it and you'll see how amazing you can feel.

Chapter Summary

1. Get clear on why you want to make changes in your health. What will it do for you? How will it make you feel? This "why" is critical to your success.

2. Think about your current beliefs around being healthy (*it's hard, it's expensive, it's boring*, etc.) and how you can shift those to new beliefs that support your goals.

3. Make a plan and start small! There doesn't need to be tons of detail, but it should be more of a plan than *I'm going to eat better*. Choose a couple of specific changes you can make to start with, get good at those, then consider adding on from there.

4. Get support. Share your goals with your family, friends, an accountability partner, or a mentor. Or all of the above! Your success is far more likely with support from someone who wants you to succeed.

5. Don't get crazy trying to decide what to eat. Include mostly unprocessed foods in your daily menu, eat the amount that makes you feel satisfied, and stick with that plan. Consistency is key.

6. Make sure to drink plenty of water. Aim for at least enough water to match half of your body weight in pounds (150 lb. = at least 75 oz. water).

7. Move your body. Whether it's walking, yoga, weightlifting, or anything else, it's important to move your body. Get your heart rate up and get sweaty!

CHAPTER SIX

Making Changes in Your Personal Finances

It's time to shift focus now and dive into money. Are you ready? To get into the right mindset, think back to why this is important in your life.

This is going to sound similar to our discussions of health. You've got to know your why and commit to it. You should have a grasp on what this means now; it is a foundation for any goal you have. No matter how big or small a goal is, you're going to come up against "stuff" that makes you want to give up. It could be a bad day, a bad week, or a bad month. If you don't have a solid reason to keep moving forward, you're dead in the water.

I read an article from Business Insider stating that Americans spend more time each year planning vacations than they do planning their financial future. I get it, because vacations are really fun to plan! But equally, I don't get it because if you carve out some time for your personal finances and your future, you can ensure you get to have more vacations to plan over the course of your life. Maybe that sounds counterintuitive, but it is the truth.

We all know what we are "supposed to" be doing to better our financial situation. Save money, spend less, make more, etc. So, what stops us? It is all based in our thoughts and our mindset.

The good news about that is that we have 100 percent control over these things. The bad news is it requires daily effort. To take control after many years of letting our thoughts and/or emotions rule us, we have to put in the work every single day. So, how do we start? Following are three steps to get you started in the right direction.

Part I: Getting Started

Know Your Why   With my finances, my why is that I like to feel secure, knowing that I have money saved for whatever life may throw in my direction. Feeling in control of my personal finances allows me to have choices and never feel stuck in my current situation (like a job I dislike) or unable to pay for important but unexpected things (car repairs, house repairs, impromptu travel to see family, medical care, etc.).

Remind yourself of your why from our earlier journaling exercises in Chapter 4. Revisit your notes and the question worksheet right now and get your why fresh in your mind. Have a clear picture of what focusing on your finances can do for your life.

Identify Your Beliefs   We already talked about our beliefs regarding our health. These beliefs are a set of principles one holds about what is right and wrong and what is true and false. Belief systems tend to be formed when we are very young, and we are usually completely unaware of them unless we do the internal work to identify them. Let's talk about money beliefs.

I like to think of different images. For our finance discussion, think about the things listed below. If you care to do a Google search and pull up other images, or grab a magazine, do that now.

a) A person dressed in high-end business attire
b) A sports car

c) A fancy dinner and a nice bottle of wine

d) A person dressed casually, maybe in workout clothes or just a T-shirt and jeans

e) A fast-food type meal

f) A basic American car

Take a few minutes to look at these different images and jot down some words or feelings that come up related to what you're seeing. There is no right or wrong here; just take note of whatever comes to mind. These words and emotions are going to give insight into your beliefs and mindset when it comes to wealth.

Just to give you some examples of mindsets or beliefs related to wealth, here are a few I've experienced myself or had others share with me:

a) Rich people are bad

b) Focusing on money is selfish

c) Making money is hard

d) I don't deserve to spend money

e) I need to earn luxurious things in life

f) Luxury items are silly

g) I'm only worthy of spending time with people at the same economic level as me

h) I don't fit in with rich people

Do any of those resonate with you? If not, think about what does resonate with you. Go back to any notes you wrote when you thought about the images I mentioned earlier. Are there any concepts repeating themselves? Did you jot down negative words or positive words? Also how did you feel internally as you looked at those images and took notes? Did you feel excited? Did you feel sad? Did you feel mad?

Did you feel something different when you considered a sports car versus a more basic car? A similar question for two people dressed in different attire: Did you like one person more than the other?

All the thoughts and emotions you noted are meaningful in identifying your existing money beliefs. If you felt more connected with the "basic" images than the "fancy" images, maybe you're feeling unworthy of the finer things in life. If you felt anger when you looked at a person in fancy clothes, maybe you feel negativity toward people who make a lot of money.

Going back to the quote I shared earlier from Eckhart Tolle: "If you get the inside right, the outside will fall into place." I want you to identify beliefs that are working against you. Get in touch with those beliefs and see how you can shift them to something more positive; you'll then be making your "inside" so much happier and supportive of your ultimate goals.

I once heard a money mindset coach talk about the energy of money, which I thought was a little crazy. *The energy of money? Money is an inanimate object, so how can it have energy?* But everything in this world is energy. These are forces we don't necessarily see, but energy is everywhere. If you think negatively about money or people who have money, yet you want to attract more money into your life, those two energies counteract each other. Having awareness of your current beliefs allows you to identify ways to shift your thinking. You can start to align your thoughts with your ultimate financial desires.

We'll look at one example of a belief and how to shift it, then you can complete the worksheet on the next page with some of your own beliefs.

Let's assume you hold the belief that making money is hard. I chose that one because it's close to my heart. I went through many years with this belief—that to make a good salary I had to work a lot of hours. I felt that lots of overtime and stress were just part of the deal if I wanted a high-paying job. Essentially, I was telling myself that I had to choose one or the other: high pay and stress or low pay and a more relaxed life. That's what I believed to be true.

So, how do you shift this belief? You can start telling yourself that money comes easily to you. You can start telling yourself that you are worthy of making "good" money, whatever that looks like for you. Even if you don't believe it right now, make a daily effort to change your thinking. Write yourself notes and put them in places you'll see on a daily basis, like your bathroom mirror, on the fridge, in your car, or even have a daily reminder set in your phone that pops up with the message "Money comes easily to me."

It takes time for new beliefs to take hold, but be consistent and it will happen. Then your daily thoughts will support your ultimate goals.

Use the worksheet on the next page or print a copy from https://tinyurl.com/GYSTbeliefsystems and write down your current beliefs and what you'd like your new beliefs to be.

Awareness of Cash Inflow and Outflow When we talk about goals related to anything—health, wealth, relationships, careers, or whatever—we need to be aware of our current situation and daily habits. When it comes to personal finances, if you're not aware of what you make and what you spend, you're walking blind. Many people are afraid to develop true insights into their financial situation because they think it will be grim. Ignoring the truth won't make it any better. Knowing where you're at now allows you to make changes to improve your situation. That's the only way to move forward.

Some of you may have the idea that understanding your finances isn't possible; that you lack the knowledge to achieve this. The only things you need to understand to have a handle on your finances are knowing how much income you bring in, what you're spending each month, and how those dollars are being spent.

MY BELIEFS ABOUT MONEY

Old Belief #1: _____
_____
_____
_____

New Belief #1: _____
_____
_____
_____

Old Belief #2: _____
_____
_____
_____

New Belief #2: _____
_____
_____
_____

Old Belief #3: _____
_____
_____
_____

New Belief #3: _____
_____
_____
_____

It may sound funny to talk about not knowing what you make; you'd think everyone knows how much money they make right? If you're a sole proprietor or business owner, your income may fluctuate month to month or you may not pay yourself on a regular basis, depending on your business model. Even if you're an employee, you may know your annual salary, but do you know exactly how much cash goes into your bank account each time you get paid? I'm talking about after tax is withheld, after insurance premiums are deducted, 401k contributions, etc., the true cash amount being deposited into your account.

No matter how you generate your income, you need to know what your income is. If you don't, that's a homework assignment for the next couple of days. Carve out some time and figure it out.

I recently heard the author-speaker Gabrielle Bernstein talk about manifesting things in life. One common thing that many people want to manifest is money. Financial abundance is on the mind of lots of people. Bernstein said something that really stuck with me; if you want to attract money to you, you'd better respect the money you've got. The principle goes that whatever you want more of, you need to put out there in the world. If you want love, give love. If you want joy, spread joy. If you want income to flow to you, spend what you've got wisely.

If you're living life with zero knowledge about your cash flow, you aren't respecting your money. Let's change that.

In terms of knowing what you spend, I've got a very straight-forward tool, a handy little spreadsheet I use to track my own cash flow. It's available to download here: https://tinyurl.com/GYSTExpense Tracker. At the most basic level, I use this to track both my monthly

Get Your Shift Together - Author Kimberly LeGrand
Expense Tracking - One week template

	Monthly	Monday	Tuesday	Wednesday
		=INPUT CELL		
	January	1-Jan	2-Jan	3-Jan
Utilities	150			
Cell phone	120			
Rent/mortgage	1,750			
Car insurance	100			
Debt payments	260			
Existing monthly savings (IRAs,	250			
Monthly contributions	50			
Health insurance	300			
Other insurance				
Groceries		50		
Meals out		10	10	10
Alcohol				
Convenient stores/coffee		5		7
Gasoline				
Entertainment				
Travel/transportation				5
Self-care (massage, pedi, etc)				
Gifts			50	
Charitable Contributions - one offs				
Medical/dental - one off expenses				
Shopping		100		
	2,980	165	60	22

Thursday	Friday	Saturday	Sunday	Monthly (weekly expenses have been extrapolated)
4-Jan	5-Jan	6-Jan	7-Jan	
				150
				120
				1,750
				100
				260
				250
				50
				300
				-
50				433
10	10	10	10	303
		35		152
	5		7	104
				-
	25			108
				22
				-
				217
	10			43
		75		325
				433
60	50	120	17	5,119

			Total income	6,000
			Net income/(expense)	**881**
			% donation	1.56%
			% savings	4.17%
			% household costs	44.67%
			% discretionary	34.93%
			Remaining cash	14.68%

income and expenses. I have a column for each day of each month, and I enter my expenses there. I have it broken down into 1) fixed expenses, such as mortgage, car payments, debt payments, insurance, and even fixed charitable contributions or fixed retirement contributions, 2) recurring nonfixed monthly expenses, such as gas and electric and cell phone bills, and 3) discretionary spending, which is everything else: coffee, meals out, groceries, gas, shopping, travel and entertainment, gifts, household items, self-care (like pedicures and massages); lots of things fall into this category. You might even include a separate line item for something like booze. You can get as detailed as you want here. I like to list major expense categories that I know have a significant monthly amount spent on them, and then a Miscellaneous category to capture one-off things. Definitely include a line item for any area you know you spend money on regularly, and any area for which you have a gut feeling you spend way more money than you think.

The idea of tracking is so that you can see, clearly in front of your face, where your money goes. I assure you, there will be some surprises. The idea is also to see if your cash inflow exceeds your outflow on a monthly basis. If it doesn't, that's the first place to start your financial planning. You've got to have inflow exceeding outflow. Then you can start to get more specific with saving money and other planning steps.

Part II: Taking Action

Once you have a clear picture of your cash flow, it's time to reflect and make some decisions. Take a look at your income compared to the various categories of expenses you have. Do this as a percentage, taking the relevant expense divided by your monthly income. If your rent or mortgage is $2,000 a month and your income is $8,000 a month, two (the expense) divided by eight (the income) gives you 0.25, which is 25 percent. Your fixed monthly housing cost is 25 percent of your monthly income. (Use my simple Excel worksheet if math isn't your forte!)

Repeat this with each of your expenses, or at least the larger expense categories. Then you can group any small items remaining into one bucket and call it "other." Once you have each of these percentages calculated, you may be surprised at what you find. Maybe you'll see that your coffee habit is a hefty chunk of your monthly income. Maybe you'll see that your daily lunch or dinner take-out habit is a larger percentage than you expected. This is exactly why going through these calculations is important. Now you really know where your money is going.

Make Some Small Shifts   Once you do this, I want you to reflect on each of these percentages you came up with. Are you surprised by any of them—either in a good way or a bad way? Look at fixed expenses, recurring nonfixed expenses, and discretionary spending. No category should be ignored.

This exercise will be different for everyone so there are no right or wrong answers. I'll caveat this whole conversation with the fact that you **need** to be in a position where your income exceeds your expenses. There are no right or wrong answers in terms of where you spend your money, but this is applicable only **after** you ensure you're not going into debt every month.

Pay attention to what emotions surface when you look at the percentages. Are there certain types of expenses that you're totally comfortable with, some that maybe give you a warm, fuzzy feeling, and others that make you feel sad or yucky? These emotions matter! They give you some guidance about where your priorities lie. The expenses that you feel good about may be areas you don't want to make changes in. The expenses that you don't feel good about are a perfect place to focus immediately.

It's important to get into the details of your personal priorities. You need to think about what expense categories give you the most bang for your buck, figuratively speaking. What makes you happy? What makes you cringe? What do you know in your heart is a waste of your money?

For a specific example, let's say you're someone who doesn't cook, doesn't want to learn to cook, and is happy with restaurants or take-out for most meals. I would say you are a person who places a high priority on the category of dining out/to-go food. You will expect to have a significant amount of spending in this category on a regular basis, let's just say 15 percent of your monthly income. Or, you may be the opposite and truly value having good quality groceries on hand at all times and making your own food at home. You'll expect to have a significant amount of spending in your grocery line item and a smaller amount in your dining-out category.

Another example is if you're someone who enjoys things like massages. I call this "self-care," but you may have another description for it. If this is you, your monthly expenses in the self-care category will be significant on a regular basis.

Another expense to look at is gifts. This may be an area where you spend way more than you think. Gifting for every occasion you can imagine is expected. If you've got kids, it's probably even worse; you have a million birthday parties and other occasions to celebrate. All. The. Time. Call me Scrooge, but a lot of times, gifting is more of a hassle than a pleasure. If you have something special in mind for someone, by all means give it to them; that is when gifting is truly enjoyable and *meaningful* for both parties. If you're just buying a gift because you feel it's the social norm, check in with yourself and decide if it's really necessary. Could a more heartfelt, less expensive (and less environmentally wasteful) gift work instead?

The reason this prioritization is important is because as you dissect your expenses, I'm going to ask you to start making decisions about where you can spend a little less. The idea here is not to cut your spending significantly (unless your cash flow situation calls for it), but rather to start with small shifts in your spending. I hear from many people that the thought of reducing expenses leads them to believe their fun will go away. This is not the case and is precisely why knowing what is most important to you and what brings you the most joy is critical. I'm not asking you to cut out your favorite things or totally change your lifestyle habits. I'm not asking you to aim for spending no money on the things you enjoy. I've read stories about some individuals who do this and are able to save enough to retire at a very early age (albeit their retirement lifestyle is generally still living in a very frugal way), but I'm not asking you to take those extreme measures. I'm asking you to have a solid awareness of where your money goes and then have a brainstorming session about where you can tweak things to get yourself in a better financial position.

Remember the book *The Compound Effect*, and how it demonstrates that seemingly inconsequential things can add up. This concept absolutely applies here. Every small amount, either saved or spent, can add up to a lot over time. Similar to our conversation around making a plan for improving your health, I'm of the opinion that in most cases, taking drastic financial measures isn't necessary; it is much more of a day-to-day lifestyle change. Ultimately, small changes over time equate to more success and a true long-term lifestyle change. You'd be surprised at the impact of small changes over time, like putting $10 a day into a savings account. That's $3,650 in a year, which is nothing to sneeze at.

The Value of Compounding a Penny   I want to share a story told in *The Compound Effect* to emphasize this concept of seemingly inconsequential action adding up to a consequential result. You may have heard this before, but it doesn't hurt to have a little reminder. Let's say you were given the choice to receive $1 million today or receive a penny doubled each day for 30 days. Which would you choose?

At first, the $1 million may feel like the right choice. Surely a penny today, doubled each day for a month, can't add up to more than that, right? Let's walk through the numbers. On Day 1 you start with $0.01. By Day 5, you're at $0.16, Day 10 is $5.12, Day 15 is $163.84. Halfway there and it's not looking good. Day 20 is $5,242.88 and Day 25 is $167,772.16. Five days left in this fun little puzzle and you've got the promise of $167,772.16 versus the $1 million you could've had 25 days ago. We are committed now, so we have to finish.

Day 26 is $335,544.32, Day 27 comes out to $671,088.64, and Day 28 is $1,342,177.28—this is where you finally break the $1 million mark, with two days left to spare! On Day 29, you've got $2,684,354.66 and then day 30 comes: $5,368,709.12. Now we're talking. A measly wait time of 30 days and you've got over $5 million in your pocket rather than $1 million. I'd wait for that!

Now, there isn't a place to put your penny today that will promise to double the value every day for 30 days, but it demonstrates that what feels like a small amount today, tomorrow, and the next day, has the ability to add up to something significant, especially with some compounding of your money.

The purpose of analyzing your finances isn't to cut out things you enjoy in life; it's to gain awareness about your financial situation.

The next time you're at the grocery store (or on Amazon) deciding what items you "need" to purchase, don't discount small dollar amounts. I know how easy it is to add small value items to your cart because *It's such a good deal, I can't say no* or because *It's only a couple bucks, so why not?* and then you get to the checkout and those little extras add up to a good chunk of change. If you're doing this over and over again, it makes a difference. Besides the financial impact of these extra purchases, you also end up with a bunch of stuff in your home that you don't really need. Having overly packed cupboards, refrigerator, and other storage areas is a cause of extra stress that I'd love each person to tackle, never mind the environmental impact, which I talk a bit about in Chapter 12.

I'm going to reemphasize here that the point of analyzing your finances isn't to cut out things you enjoy in life. It isn't to make you think really hard about every dollar you spend. Just like obsessing over every bite of food you take can be damaging in the long run, obsessing over every penny spent can also be damaging and make life not very fun. The goal is to gain awareness about your financial inflows and outflows, analyze what you find, and decide where you can make some small shifts in your current habits to better your personal financial situation. Once you have a good framework in place, you then have ... freedom. We already touched on this freedom in Chapter 3.

I know I've talked a lot about small day-to-day spending like on coffee and food. Those are the easy categories to tackle. They're often categories that end up surprising you when you calculate how much money you spend each month. However, you must also look at your recurring monthly expenditures; cell phone, internet, cable, car insurance, and other monthly services. Pull out your last couple of credit card or debit card statements and look through all monthly expenditures. Make sure you're capturing everything. I bet some of you will find monthly subscriptions that you forgot about and no longer care to pay for. Take care of those first! That is low hanging fruit, so to speak. Call or email the company you've been paying **today** and cancel the autopay right away. That's money flowing out the door for no reason.

For other monthly expenditures that are necessary, like car insurance, consider how long you've had the policy in place. If it's been more than two years, revisit it. Shop around. Think about whether your circumstances have changed, either how much you drive, where you live, or how long it's been since you've had any incidents on your driving record (e.g., a speeding ticket or accident.) This could be an area for savings. I know it is super boring, but what if you can reduce your expense even just $200 a year? Put the time and effort in once, then reap the rewards time after time. Doesn't that sound nice?

Let's also talk about home internet and cable. I take these together since they're often bundled. This is definitely a hot button for me. First of all, the cost of cable TV is ridiculous. Second of all, I'm not a huge TV person, but when I do watch, it's rarely cable channels. Most of the shows I gravitate to are on the good ol' standard local channels. Thinking about our conversation on priorities, this is a low-priority category for me. If you feel similarly or are in need of reducing your expenses quickly, this is an area to tackle. Research what other options are available in your area. I'm not a techy person so I won't give specifics here, but I know there are ways to get rid of cable altogether if you want to. I'm sure you have a friend or family member who is knowledgeable about this kind of thing. Ask for help. What if you could save $100 a month? That's $1,200 a year; $6,000 over five years. Hello, compound effect! And it's saving in a category that doesn't bring you a lot of joy anyway. Save those hard-earned dollars for things that add value to your life. Even if this is a high priority category for you, look at ways to cut your current bill. Often, these kinds of expenses creep up over time without you noticing.

Finally, look at your fixed expenses. These expenses probably feel like necessities, such as rent or your mortgage, which they likely are, but don't ignore them. These generally make up the largest portion of your monthly expenses percentagewise. Look through each of the items that make up this category and consider if there's any room to save on them. For housing costs, maybe there's a way to save by moving somewhere a bit cheaper. I'm not saying to uproot yourself just to save a few bucks, but depending on how much you love where you live, maybe there's an opportunity for cheaper rent somehow. With a mortgage, have you thought about refinancing your loan? It doesn't hurt to talk to a couple of lenders.

With other fixed expenses, like a car payment, ask yourself if you are spending within your means. This is an area where your priorities come into play. For me, I don't place any importance on what kind of car I drive. I just want to get safely from point A to point B. Other people feel differently. As long as the amount of money you're spending makes sense in your own income/expense situation, anything is okay. But I'm challenging you to think hard about where all your money is going. You may be in a car lease that seemed like a good idea at the time but is now sucking up a lot of your monthly cash flow.

I want you to go through and dissect each of your major spending categories. Make decisions about where you want to cut costs and commit to doing it. If you share finances with a partner, do this together. You've got to be on the same page or it's not going to work. This may mean some compromise for both parties, but that's what being in a relationship is all about. Use Part III of this chapter to guide these conversations.

Start Saving All right, you knew that eventually we had to get to the subject of saving. Here we go! I've heard different statistics over the years regarding Americans and savings. A 2019 survey by GOBankingRates, who has been doing a similar survey since 2014, reported the following:

1. 45% of respondents have $0 in savings
2. 69% of respondents (including the 45% above) have $1,000 or less in savings
3. Top reasons respondents aren't saving more is (a) living paycheck to paycheck and (b) high cost of living
4. The number one way respondents said they would be able to save more is to earn a higher salary

You can search Google and find plenty of other statistics about savings. I don't know any of the individuals who completed this survey, and I don't claim to be a perfect saver myself, but I truly believe that many people who currently save nothing could start saving right now. It may not be much, but even a little bit each month builds up to something worthwhile. You cannot wait until you earn more money to start saving. I assure you, if you're not saving now, when you start to earn more, you're not going to save then either, simply because you don't have a plan in place.

I realize I was fortunate in my upbringing. Learning about money from my parents was a huge blessing. Not everybody has this. However, I want to instill hope that no matter where you are today, you can start saving and improve your financial future. Saving is important for a number of reasons, so let's dive into them.

You can't predict what will happen in the future, and you can't assume the income you have now will be there as long as you need it. You've got to save for the unexpected.

We're all aware that circumstances can change overnight. Businesses may suddenly lose their usual stream of income. Employees can lose the job they so fiercely relied on for survival, leaving them unable to pay their rent. It has happened quickly in the past, whether on a global or local scale, without real warning, and could happen again. Whatever situation you're in at the moment—whether good or bad—is not permanent. *You need to save money.*

So, how do you start? If you're not saving anything right now, start small. Make a commitment to save a small amount monthly or out of each paycheck. Maybe that's $50 biweekly or $100 monthly. If that is too much for right now, pick a number you know you can manage. Remember, there's no cookie cutter plan right for everyone.

If you are an employee, a lot of companies make it easy to save by giving you the option to have a specific amount of each paycheck deposited somewhere other than your checking account. If you're truly committed to this savings plan, then go ahead and do this! It literally makes it impossible for you to fail at saving. As I've said before, I'm a huge fan of taking the decision-making and effort out of anything you possibly can.

If you're not an employee, many banks have online banking options where you can set up an automatic transfer from one account to another. I do this monthly with a certain amount and contribute it to my IRA (individual retirement account). I set it up once and I never have to think about it. It just happens.

How do you know what the right amount is? Look back at your expense tracking. Hopefully, you have at least a full month of data to work with. Where are you at the end of the month? If you've got negative cash flow (meaning your expenses exceed your income), first get that number to a positive by following the steps given earlier in this book. That is your number one priority. Once you have a positive figure, then I'd say shoot for $50 to $100 a month in savings to start.

If you're already in the black (meaning your income exceeds your expenses), pick an amount that's at least 5 percent of your income. That's a good starting point if you've never saved and you can work up from there. If you've got room to save more than that, do it!

Then, once this savings account has started, leave it alone unless there's a true need for it.

What Are You Saving For? If you want to know more about why you should save, I'll give you two good reasons.

Short-term safety net. It's important to have some cash on hand for surprise expenditures. I like the idea of having cash to cover six months' worth of expenses.

Maybe an unexpected expense comes up for your car, home or even a medical bill. You don't want to put this on a credit card; it becomes exponentially more expensive if you don't pay that credit card off immediately.

Sometimes, unexpected things happen with your income and you need extra cash. Let's say you have a seasonal business and you're in a slow season. This is something you want to plan for and know that you'll be okay. Another example is if your company goes through restructuring and you wind up without that paycheck you thought was so secure. If you've got cash in the bank, this is far less stressful. A cutback or layoff is already emotionally stressful, so make it easier on yourself by removing the fear of not being able to pay your bills while you search for a new job.

My favorite thing to talk about regarding short-term safety nets is breathing room. Let's say you're wanting to change jobs or leave your job to start your own business. These can both be really exciting things! What can make it even more exciting is if you have some cash to get you through the transition. I've changed jobs many times and I've also gone from being an employee to self-employed. When I was changing jobs, it was fantastic to know that I could take a bit of time off between jobs. When else do you get this opportunity? Who wants to go from working your tail off in one job to jumping into another one immediately, one where you're going to need to be on point making a great first impression with your new colleagues? Give yourself at least a one- or two-week break. You can't even contemplate this if you have no cash to get through a couple weeks without pay.

Alternatively, if you're transitioning from a salaried position to working for yourself, it's likely there will be a period of time between receiving your final paycheck and earning steady income from your new business. You can make this less stressful by having some cash in the bank.

Choices. Going through life having more choices is so much better than feeling like you're handcuffed due to not having enough money. Am I talking about having the choice between a private jet or a luxury yacht to get to you Bora Bora? Maybe for some of you reading this, that's a choice you're looking to make. For the most part, though, I'm talking about choices you make in your day-to-day life about regular day-to-day stuff.

One example of this is childcare. As a new mom, I am already dealing with this and it's not going away anytime soon. Childcare is expensive! Whether that's an in-home nanny, daycare, or even just having a babysitter occasionally, the expense of this adds up quickly. With many parents working full-time, budgeting for childcare expenses is a necessity. When it comes time to make decisions about childcare, wouldn't you love to have more choices? Maybe the option you really want is not something you can afford with your current income and expenses. What if you had some savings you could dip into to help out with this? This is what I'm talking about in terms of choices. I know many families don't have the ability to make the choices they'd really like to. When it comes to your kids, that's heartbreaking. Even having the option to have a babysitter once in a while to give mom or dad a break can be life-changing (or at least sanity-saving). When it comes to these kinds of decisions, the $50 spent on a babysitter so that mom can have some time to herself or to allow the parents to have time together is much more meaningful than dropping $50 on impulse purchases at the store or an extra bottle of wine at dinner out.

Having some savings takes the pressure off yourself financially. With a little bit of planning around your personal finances, you can relieve some of the pressure you find yourself under when making decisions about important normal life stuff.

Keep in mind, though, that anytime you dip into your short-term safety net (which should only be for truly important things), the next step is replenishing it to get back to six months' worth of expenses.

Random Money Let me explain what I mean by "random money." This is money that comes into your bank account outside your normal sources of income. This can include monetary gifts for a birthday, getting a refund from the IRS for income tax, inheriting money, cash made from some lucky hands of cards in Las Vegas, or a bonus from your employer. You get the idea.

What do you do with random money when it comes to you? To get you in the right frame of mind for this discussion, pretend for a moment that you unexpectedly receive $2,000 of random money. You may be thinking: *Yay, that's exciting! What am I going to do with this money?* Now jot down the first couple of things that come to mind. Are your ideas along the lines of spending this money on something? A cool trip, that TV you've been eyeing, the latest phone, clothes, some new equipment for your home gym, or a DIY project? Or, are your ideas along the lines of saving this money or paying down some debt? Maybe your thoughts are a combination. Nothing you jotted down is wrong. I'm not here to add any guilt to how you spend your money. But I want you to be aware of where your mind immediately goes when you think about coming into unexpected money.

For me, random money is always an opportunity to save or pay off some kind of debt (extra principal on your mortgage?). That doesn't mean the entire amount is used in this way, but assuming the amount we're talking about is over, say $250, I never have the intention of going out and spending 100 percent of it. Save it or pay off debt.

Spending on Credit Cards   The subject of credit cards can be a touchy one. I've heard many people talk about credit card companies as evil. I agree that you can get yourself in a lot of trouble with credit cards; those companies are out to make money. That's their business! But I don't agree that credit cards are evil; if you use them in a smart way, they are fabulous tools and can come with great benefits.

The key here is *if you use them in a smart way.* My hope is that after you go through all the steps I've outlined regarding your personal finances, you are in a position to be one of those people who benefits from a credit card, rather than being used by the credit card company.

My favorite things about a credit card are:

1. You can borrow money for free
2. There can be great perks like cash back, air miles, or other travel benefits
3. They are safer in terms of someone being able to access your actual cash (like a debit card) versus a line of credit (with a credit card)

If you're going to use a credit card, here are my basic rules:

1. First and foremost, you *always* pay your full balance off, on time, every month. By doing this, you aren't paying any interest on the amount you've technically "borrowed" for a short time. You're borrowing for free for anywhere from 30–60 days.
2. Look at your credit card statement every month and act on anything you don't recognize or didn't authorize; this includes auto-subscriptions that you did allow but you don't want/need anymore.

With this said, if you can't follow rule number one, forget using a credit card. Stick with cash and a debit card, but you better still be following rule number two with your debit card statements no matter what.

Here is a quick example of how interest on credit cards can get you. Assume you charge $500 on your credit card for some new clothes and pay off the minimum balance each month and are charged an interest rate of 20 percent. You would make over 100 payments (that's nine years) and pay an additional $584 in interest. You just more than doubled the cost of those clothes—clothes you may not even own nine years after the original purchase. Now, let's assume you charged $2,000 on your card under the same interest rate and payment requirements. For this amount, you would make over 500 payments (almost 44 years) and pay an additional $8,084 in interest. This time, you've *quadrupled* the cost of whatever was purchased on your credit card. Yikes! Remember this when you're booking that vacation or buying something that you so desperately "need" but know you won't be able to pay off without incurring interest.

I realize that conversations about money trigger anxiety and other negative emotions for many people. This can stem from different experiences and belief systems, but some of that negativity comes from the unknown; like you are in the dark about your personal financial situation. If you're feeling like you don't know enough about money to make any changes for yourself, believe me (a CPA) when I tell you that you don't need to know anything more than what we've just talked about. What I've outlined in this discussion is doable for anyone! It's not rocket science to take small action steps, to become aware of your income and your expenses, and then analyze what that looks like now versus how you'd like it to look. It does take some time and a little bit of organization, but you are worth that investment. Your sanity and happiness are worth that investment.

Part III: Planning with a Partner

Talk, Talk, Talk　　Relationships add a whole new dimension to money conversations. It's one thing when you're totally in control of your own money; it's something else when you've got to make decisions with another person. Rarely will your thoughts and values on money line up exactly with your significant other's thoughts and values. Opposites do tend to attract. If you're in a relationship, even if you're not at the stage of combining your finances, please commit to going through this entire money section of the book with your partner. You will learn so much about each other and it will help you flush out some of the areas that each of you place importance on and areas where you're each willing to compromise.

Talking about money isn't going to be a one-time occurrence. You and your partner need to commit to talking about this often, whether that's a scheduled time weekly/monthly or when new expenses come up or income situations change.

When you're first having these conversations, commit to talking until you're both comfortable with a baseline plan for how your joint money will be handled. Then you can just talk as needed, other than an occasional chat to check in on how you're both doing.

Commit to being transparent. This will not work if you or your partner are hiding things, whether that's income or expenses.

Commit to being honest. This will not work if either person holds back in saying exactly what they need to be on board with the final plan.

Bottom line: there needs to be a lot talking! Money is an emotional and controversial subject, so be open to listening to your partner, know where you stand in terms of your own values and non-negotiables, and be ready for compromise on both sides.

My Personal Story   I was raised in a household where we talked about money. I learned early on that credit card debt was not the way to go and to pay attention to how much things cost. I know this isn't very common, so I'm forever grateful for this early education. Once I was out on my own after college and making a decent income, I already had a good foundation to avoid getting into credit card debt and continue saving.

In my mid-20s, when I started dating my now ex-husband, new challenges arose. We had different philosophies on finances, but being young and in love, I figured the differences could be worked around.

We talked about money and our own values, but not nearly enough. Money conversations are tough. I didn't want money to be the center of our relationship, and I didn't want to "impose" my own views on another person. The funny thing about that is that by ignoring the tough conversations, this made money end up being at the center of our relationship. There's a saying that *what you resist persists*, and it's spot on. Finances ended up being a very contentious point in our marriage and contributed to its eventual demise.

Options for Planning   I've heard couples talk about not combining finances at all, combining them partially, or combining them fully. I've also heard of having fully combined finances, but then deciding on a specific monthly amount that each person gets to have as personal funds, so to speak, and they can choose what to do with that money; almost like an allowance. There is no right or wrong answer here, but ultimately, you both need to be comfortable with the plan.

If there are kids in the picture, having fully separate finances isn't a viable option, so leave that one alone.

Designate one person to be the primary money person. Typically, one person gravitates more to money, so this is often an easy decision. Keep in mind this is not a position of power, but of responsibility.

No matter what the earnings are for each person, you are equals when you're talking about your joint financial picture. If you're a stay-at-home mom, you have equal say in the family finances. Being a mom is a job, it's just unpaid. Don't think for one second that it takes away your right to be a part of money discussions or decisions.

The most straightforward way to plan your joint finances is to fully combine all earnings and expenses into one place. This gives you full visibility of your family's financial picture. Use the spreadsheet I created and tweak it for your own situation. Get a clear picture of each person's spending habits and then talk through each category. If you're spending more than you're making as a couple, step one is to get that fixed. This means evaluating all expenses and figuring out what can be cut. I guarantee there are areas where spending can be reduced without significantly impacting your lifestyle.

As soon as you are in the position of having a positive cash flow each month, decide how much you want to save. First look at building up short-term savings, aiming for six months' worth of expenses. Next, look at long-term savings, for you as a couple, and for your kids. As soon as you know how much you want to save each month, work out how to make that happen. It may mean cutting some additional expenses, but don't adjust your savings goal to fit your personal spending desires. Look at it from the other direction. Obviously, you need to cover essential living expenses, but you also need to save.

If only one person in the relationship has income, this needs to be discussed. I know from personal experience and hearing from lots of moms, this can be tricky. Sometimes, the income earner doesn't appreciate the expenses that come along with children, or the full-time parent doesn't feel comfortable spending money or feels limited in decision-making power. Each person's view deserves to be heard and ultimately you, as a couple, need to decide what works for you.

Chapter Summary

1. Get clear on why you want to improve your financial situation. What will this do for you? How will it make you feel? This "why" is critical to your success.

2. Identify your current beliefs about finances (*Making money is hard; Gaining wealth is bad; I don't "need" more money*) and consider how you can shift those beliefs to support your goals. Use the worksheet included in this chapter.

3. Gain awareness of your current financial situation. Use the expense tracker provided to record and review your income and expenses. Even if this step scares you, awareness is key!

4. If your expenses exceed your income, decide which expenses you can reduce to fix this. You can't be in a position of consistently spending more than you make! If your income exceeds your expenses, decide on a couple of small shifts you can make to your current expenses to better your financial position.

5. Decide on an amount you can save monthly and implement a plan to make this savings easy for you (automatically via a paycheck deduction or via transfers between bank accounts). Start small and work from there.

6. If you have a significant other, include them in this planning, especially if you have children together. You're going to need to talk a lot; be prepared with your own views on what is important, and be ready to compromise. Refer to Part III of this chapter for more guidance.

CHAPTER SEVEN

The Downfall of Shortcuts

Now that we've been through the tactical approach to improving your health and finances, your brain may start trying to make plans of how to get from A to B quickly. Remember, this is a long-term plan!

If you want lasting success in anything, there is no shortcut. Shortcuts can get you results, and there may be a time and a place for them, but you don't learn anything; therefore, when you come up against new challenges, you don't have the skills to overcome them. The idea is to strengthen your own skill set—learn discipline, increase your knowledge base, show yourself how strong you are, and be forced to work through the emotions that come up along your journey. Once you have been through the process of shifting your habits, you show yourself that you can get through anything life throws your way.

Instant Gratification

Instant gratification is the way of the world these days. Talking about it gets me really fired up, and not in a good way. Society has consistently moved in the direction of making things immediately available. Interest-free financing to buy things you can't really afford. Loans against your future tax refunds or paychecks to buy things now. Drive-through ... everything. Take-out food delivered straight to your car by a friendly employee (because, heaven forbid, you have to get out of your car and walk a few steps to get it). Mobile order your favorite coffee so you can bypass a line in the coffee shop. Same-day delivery for groceries and anything you can possibly imagine from Amazon. Electronic communications rather than snail mail.

I can't deny that I enjoy some of these conveniences and I absolutely hate waiting in lines. My problem with this instant gratification thought process is that as we get used to these conveniences with some of our daily activities, it bleeds into all areas of our life. *If I can get my morning coffee without waiting, how come I can't lose weight without waiting? If I can order my lunch online in 30 seconds and have it ready for me to pick up and eat five minutes later, why would I spend 20 minutes in the morning packing a lunch for myself? If I can put something on a credit card and pay it off over the next five years, why would I save for six to 12 months and then buy it with cash?* This creates a constant desire for having what we want now. It makes us feel like having to wait for or spend time on anything (like cooking, or even sleeping) is too much to ask. I also believe it causes more stress rather than reducing it.

When we eliminate certain time-sucking things in our lives, like waiting in line or having to go to a physical brick and mortar store to buy household items, the immediate benefit is saving time. Now, the question is *What do we use that saved time for instead?* The vast majority of us probably would admit that saved time isn't used on our well-being, such as going to bed earlier, cooking fresh food, having some quiet time with a book, spending quality time with a loved one, or getting outside for some movement. As we eliminate the need to spend time on certain boring things, we end up packing our day with even more tasks. More kids' activities, more work calls or meetings, more socializing, or more shopping trips to buy random stuff to junk up our lives. Maybe this saved time simply equates to more time in front of the television. I'm sure I sound like a grumpy old lady by saying this, but I do have a strong opinion about the pace at which many people are living and the typical level of consumerism. To each their own, but it's important for every person to have quiet time with their own thoughts and having a lot of "stuff" gets in the way of living our best life.

When we get used to instant communication methods like emails and texts, people come to expect immediate replies at all times of the day or night which can be quite stressful. I recall once working with a client in India, which is in a significantly different time zone than California. There were several times during that project that the team in India proposed having calls at 9 or 10 PM my time. To me, unless there is a very important deadline looming, there is no reason for work calls at that time.

At this same job, I asked one of my superiors—who had been in the industry for his entire career—about his life outside of work, and he shared that he *used* to have time to serve on boards and be involved in the local community. He said that with the ever-increasing work-load on him and the other executives, there wasn't much time to be active in anything else. That was a nugget of information I held onto as I decided on my next career move.

Nothing achieved via shortcuts teaches you anything about facing and overcoming challenges.

How does all this instant gratification talk tie in with our discussion about working on our goals? By living our lives in this mode of expecting things now, we also want results from health eating, exercising, saving money, working hard in our careers NOW. It doesn't work like that. Anything worth doing takes time. Nothing achieved via shortcuts (or without effort) teaches you anything about facing and overcoming inevitable challenges.

Weight Loss Shortcuts

A tempting approach to weight loss that's widely marketed is consuming special pills, powders, or teas—all of these claim that they'll help burn fat, suppress appetite, or speed up metabolism. I've tried a few over the course of my life, so I'm not judging these approaches. The promise that something will help shed pounds or suppress your appetite without having to change your habits is very appealing. How much easier could it be? There are two things to think about before you decide to go down this route.

First, *is the product safe?* I can't answer this for you and honestly, the product manufacturer might not really know this either—they don't know you or your specific health circumstances, so how can they know *for sure* that something is safe for *you?* Some companies do care about your health, but most are all about profits. This goes for many food manufacturers as well. There is plenty of evidence to show that ingredients used in processed "foods" are not good for us, yet manufacturers keep the conveyor belts pumping out those products day and night. The bottom line with safety is that you just don't know the true impact something will have on you, so think about this before you decide to take any supplement touting weight loss benefits.

The second thing to think about is *longevity.* If you start taking something to help with weight loss or appetite control, are you willing to take it forever? If not, it might help you while you're taking it, but whenever you don't care to pay for it anymore, what happens then? You're back to square one. This is why focusing on the real solution—

healthy food, daily movement, hydration, and sleep—always wins! If you put in the work to get good daily habits in place, you are set forever.

My Own Weight Loss Journey

During my college years, after I gained the freshman fifteen—the weight college freshmen often gain in their first year away from home—I was determined to lose it and get back to feeling healthy and fitting into my clothes. I was already 10–15 pounds heavier than I needed to be when I started college, so I had a good amount of weight to lose.

Once I was committed to losing the weight, I decided how I would approach it. The two things I knew I could control immediately were watching my nutrition and getting active. I met with a nutritionist a couple of times to get grounded and soak up advice from an expert. I made healthier choices in the dining hall, which wasn't always easy since there were so many unhealthy choices alongside healthy ones. Hello mac and cheese, pizza, or chicken tenders and french fries! Hello brownie à la mode, one of my favorite desserts! I made conscious decisions to choose vegetables, healthy carbohydrates, and lean proteins, rather than fat- and sodium-laden foods. I also made meals for myself in my dorm room when possible and used the college gym four or five times a week. Talk about a super simple plan, huh? I stuck to this approach consistently through my college years. When I say consistently, I mean most of the time. Nobody is perfect and perfection isn't the goal. You've got to leave room to stray from your plan and sleep through your normal workout time once in a while. Life is meant to be enjoyed.

By the time I graduated, I was about ten pounds lighter than when I started college. Now, you may read this and think, *Wow, it took*

you a whole three to four years to get rid of that weight? That's a long time.
Could I have done it quicker? Yes! Could I have been stricter on my
diet to make it happen faster? Yes! There are a lot of ways I could've lost
the weight in a shorter time frame, but the way I did it made it man-
ageable for me. I didn't have to change my lifestyle completely. I didn't
have to give up eating out. I didn't have to become a three-hours-a-day
gym rat. And best of all, I haven't gained weight since then!

From age 22 to now at 41, I've never put that weight back on (with
the exception of my pregnancy, of course), and in fact, I've lost more
weight by really focusing on my nutrition and fitness plan. This, my
friend, is what I want for you. It's not that I want you to have my exact
journey; I want you to learn ways to shift habits that you can carry
with you forever. There's no way a quick fix or shortcut would've given
me the same results. It doesn't need to be about the weight, either.
It's about feeling good in your skin and being in overall good health,
whatever that means for you.

Fad Diets

Looking further at this reason for skipping "shortcut" plans, take
someone who follows all the latest fad diets, switching from paleo to
keto to celery juice to cabbage soup to raw, based on whatever is trend-
ing at that time. We all know people who do this, maybe you're one of
them. I pass no judgment whatsoever on this approach. Because of
the way these diets are advertised, it's very appealing to give them a
try. Generally speaking, though, they aren't sustainable, and as you
know by now, I don't go for that. So, let's say this person loses a few
pounds from following a specific diet plan for a month. That's great!
They feel amazing and successful. Then, life happens and they loosen
up their "rules" a little bit and weight starts to return. This is going
to happen no matter what. Trust me. A few years ago, I thought I

had it all figured out and would never struggle with self-discipline ever again. Wrong. Life is a fluid journey and you'll have different phases where you're more disciplined and phases where you're less disciplined.

What does the person who chooses a fad diet do after they've loosened up their rules so much that they feel out of control? Since that last fad diet didn't work out for them, they pick another fad diet and hope that it kicks them back into gear. Everyone I know who does this has great fluctuations in their weight, and never gets to the point of feeling in control of their health.

There are times you don't feel so amazing and struggle with self-discipline, injuries, or sickness. However, when you know how to get back on track through healthy habits, setbacks aren't so devastating.

It's also important to consider how transferable your way of eating is—the ease in which you are able to eat even when having dinner at a friend's house, going away for a weekend, or traveling outside of your own country. I've been around people who lug a bunch of food with them wherever they go so that they can have exactly what they usually eat at home. If this works for you, more power to you. But, for me, this makes going anywhere a total pain in the rear end, can be anxiety producing, and definitely not as much fun. I'll admit that I've taken my own food when having dinner with certain friends or family so that they don't need to worry about having vegetarian/vegan options available for me. This is a personal choice I make to ease the burden on my loved ones when I think it's appropriate. I recognize there are also certain digestive and/or allergy reasons why a person may need to bring their own food with them, but the idea is to make the way you eat as easy as possible for your situation so that it doesn't require so much dang planning.

It's a Marathon, Not a Sprint

Something I've learned in the last couple of years is that our health is truly a journey, not a destination. It's not a linear path. There are times you feel amazing and are very disciplined in your nutrition and fitness routine. There are times you don't feel so amazing and struggle with self-discipline. There are times that setbacks present themselves, like an injury, sickness, or other medical condition. However, when you know how to get back on track through healthy practices, setbacks aren't so devastating. This is exactly why it's important to lean on good habits rather than quick fixes. You also don't panic about being off your normal routine while you're on vacation or on your birthday or even just for fun on any given day. I love pizza and will never give it up. I love chocolate and will never give it up. You don't have to give up anything when you have a good foundation.

A prime example: my pregnancy experience. I had some great new experiences with highs and lows in my personal health journey while pregnant, and now post-partum.

In my first trimester, I experienced food aversions, sometimes to all foods, especially vegetables. I also had very low energy so workouts were a drag! I did my best to stay active (albeit at a lower intensity) and eat as many healthy foods as I could stomach. This only worked because I already had solid habits in place.

My second and third trimesters were tolerable until the final few weeks, when I developed an insatiable appetite. My breakfast was never enough. I still wanted just one more bite of something. I never felt full. I wanted to snack all the time. It was wild! But, I did my best to find healthy snacks like dried edamame, crunchy broad beans (the brand "Bada Bean Bada Boom" was my best friend), peanut butter filled pretzels, and raw nuts with unsweetened dried fruit.

Despite feeling like I was eating everything in sight throughout my pregnancy, I was grateful that I already had healthy eating habits. If I didn't, it would've been easy to slip into eating a whole lot of crap. Habits are what carry you through inevitable challenges in life. They allow you to face these challenges and not get completely derailed from your goals. We don't have control of very many things in life, but what we do have control over is our own actions. That's about it. Let's get really good at taking action in the direction of the life we've envisioned for ourselves.

Forget the Financial Shortcuts

I know I've focused on health in this chapter, but it's applicable to your financial situation as well. There's no fast track to being financially sound. Sure, you may hear about individuals or companies that are very successful and think, *Wow, they must be very smart* or *They must have had the most amazing idea.* You may meet people in your day-to-day life that seem like they "have it together" financially, whatever that looks like for you. However, behind every successful entity or individual, I promise you there are many, many hours (probably years) of hard work and a lot of failure along the way. There are no successful get-rich-quick plans.

Here are a few of the famous "failures" that became successes: Author J. K. Rowling was a single mother on welfare when she wrote her first book, *Harry Potter and the Sorcerer's Stone.* She was writing mostly in cafés while her daughter napped. She was rejected by twelve publishers before a small publishing house agreed to publish her book. Bill Gates, one of the wealthiest individuals in the world, had his first company fail. Walt Disney was fired from a job for lacking creativity.

There are plenty of examples of regular people too. People who consistently save, monitor their expenses, and spend time each year evaluating their financial situation. These people do the small things on a daily basis that add up to a nice retirement nest egg down the road.

Don't waste your brain space on hoping to win the lottery, getting a big inheritance, or being awarded money through a lawsuit. Maybe those are possible for you, but is that the way you want to live? Hoping that someday, somehow, a big chunk of change shows up in your bank account from one of those unlikely avenues? Your likelihood of success—and your own mental health—is better if you cut out that kind of thinking and take control of your own financial situation.

When you look at your goals and think about the changes required, see them as lifestyle changes. That doesn't mean a week or a month or three months. It means for *life!* That can seem overwhelming, I know. That's why I'm a fan of skipping crazy, extreme methods, and setting small, realistic goals. Understand your finances and take baby steps to build the future you want. You won't become a millionaire overnight, but you'll learn about money and gain important skills.

Chapter Summary

Shortcuts don't teach you anything. Learn to overcome challenges with a plan that may take longer, but will give you lasting results. Remember, this is about lifestyle changes that are going to give you exactly what you've always wanted!

CHAPTER EIGHT

Don't Worry About What Everyone Else Is Doing

You might have heard the phrase "comparison is the thief of joy." It's the truth. Not comparing ourselves with others is also one of the hardest things to do, especially in this age of social media. We are inundated with images of toned bodies, posts about how much money someone makes, what kind of lifestyle they're leading, cool travel pictures, lovey-dovey family photos, and all kinds of opinions about everything. It can be challenging to escape.

Don't get me wrong—I'm not a hater of travel and family posts—they're fun to see and people have a right to share whatever they feel like sharing on their social media pages. But, if you're indulging in what you see in these posts, it's tough not to compare yourself. If you can stop worrying about other people, you'll be amazed at how much better you feel. Also, bear in mind that anything you see or hear may be completely misleading. You never know the whole truth behind a social media post. Has that person been photoshopped? Is that person as happy as they look? Is that person really making as much money as it sounds? You'll never know the truth, and at the end of the day, it shouldn't matter to *you*! It's not worth using up brain space on that. Focus on *your* vision and *your* plan.

I was watching an episode of the Netflix series *Down to Earth* hosted by actor Zac Efron and superfood hunter Darin Olein, as they were talking with some long-time residents of a small town in Sardinia, Italy. Sardinia is one of the world's Blue Zones, meaning they have a high percentage of individuals who live to 100 or beyond. One thing that hit me as I watched this was how living somewhere less commercialized, more remote, and with fewer people could be such an amazing experience. This town was beautiful, and I imagine the people featured—who were all in their late 90s—appreciated its beauty. They weren't scrolling their Facebook or Instagram feeds seeing what everyone else was up to. They were taking walks, spending time with family, visiting friends, and even having a glass of wine at their local bar. I imagine these people weren't sitting around longing for some other life, somewhere else.

As individuals, we get to decide for ourselves what is best and what makes us happy. Each person is different. Each body is different. Each life is meant to be lived differently. Each person is called to do different things in life. We were not meant to all act or look a certain way. How boring would that be, anyway?

> **Appreciation is a wonderful thing. It makes what is excellent in others belong to us as well.**
> —VOLTAIRE

If you see someone leaner or stronger or with a rounder butt than you, be happy for them! If you and a friend are doing a nutrition challenge together and your friend ends up getting results more quickly, celebrate with them! If you meet someone who makes more money than you or owns a car or house that you would love to have, be stoked for that person. I participated in a manifestation challenge that the author Gabrielle Bernstein offered, and I want to share something she discussed in one of her lessons: when you can be happy for others who have something you want, this helps attract that very thing into your life. Don't be jealous of others or allow yourself to feel bad about where you're at on your journey. Celebrate other people's successes, knowing that you are focused on making improvements in your own life to achieve something similar. As long as you are taking action toward your own goals, this becomes easy.

You know your mind and body better than anyone else. Decide for yourself how you want to eat, what kind of exercise you want to do. Decide for yourself what being healthy means, what kind of a lifestyle you want. Decide for yourself what kind of a financial position you want to be in and what success means. Then, don't worry about anybody else's view. Stay grounded in your own values so no matter what influences come your direction, you can't be swayed. If you are unsure of how to go about things, you can always discuss your goals with a professional—a nutritionist or personal trainer to get input on your health. Speak to a financial adviser about your financial situation. Don't take advice from people who aren't qualified or those who don't have the same end goals as you. Sure, you can learn from people about what they've tried and what they like, but it may not be the same situation or work the same for you. This quote sums it up nicely:

> It is not the critic who counts; not the man who points
> out how the strong man stumbles, or where the doer
> of deeds could have done them better. The credit
> belongs to the man who is actually in the arena,
> whose face is marred by dust and sweat and blood;
> who strives valiantly; who errs, who comes short again
> and again, because there is no effort without error and

shortcoming; but who does actually strive to do the
deeds; who knows great enthusiasms, the great
devotions; who spends himself in a worthy cause; who
at the best, knows in the end the triumph of high
achievement, and who at the worst, if he fails, at least
fails while daring greatly so that his place shall never
be with those cold and timid souls who neither know
victory nor defeat.
—THEODORE ROOSEVELT

Make sure you only take advice from people who know what
you're going for and have relevant experience that applies to your situation. Even then, sometimes you just need to trust yourself.

Chapter Summary
1. Comparison is the thief of joy. Practice focusing on yourself
   and your own journey, without comparing yourself to
   others.
2. Only take advice from people who have relevant knowledge and experience for what you want to get out of life.
   Even then, you are the only one who really knows the
   right answer.

CHAPTER NINE

Navigating Life as a Parent

For all the parents reading this book, I want to give you some things to focus on and some words of wisdom and hope. Parenting does change your life. It changes your priorities, your free time, your expenses, and many other things. Parenting does not mean you don't have the ability or right to still take care of yourself and your finances. It is tougher to focus on these things, but it's important and not impossible.

Change in Focus

While writing this book, I became pregnant and now have a beautiful baby girl. Being a mom has changed my approach to health. I now have more commitment to healthy living, because I want to be around for a very long time to see my baby girl grow up. This commitment has shifted more toward overall health rather than just trying to look good in a bikini. I also want to teach my daughter healthy habits so that she has a good foundation for when she spreads her wings and goes off on her own. After all, our kiddos learn a significant part of the beliefs that shape their life by the age of about five. That means that teaching by example needs to start right out of the gate!

Having a child has made me more aware of how my husband and I talk about food, how I talk about my body, and how quickly I eat. I know my daughter is always watching and listening. If I'm shoveling my lunch into my face in two minutes flat while standing at the kitchen counter, what will my daughter learn? These are the things I now think about as I go through my day. Not that those eating methods are completely unacceptable, but I don't like them to be the norm. I want her to know that eating meals is not just important for her, but it's important for me too. If she gets older and starts to witness me not taking the time to care for myself, she may get the idea that if/when she ever becomes a mom, she doesn't deserve to take care of herself either. That's not the example I want to set.

If you are thinking there is no choice in the matter when you have little ones at home, hear me out. Yes, it's busy and crazy (and I only have one child, so I'm no parenting expert). Yes, there are going to be times that you have to make some sacrifices just to survive. If you can keep in mind that you are important and that your child is learning from you about what "grown-up" life might be like for them, this will support you in taking care of yourself the way you deserve.

Priorities

Once there are one or more little humans in the picture, different priorities for your precious resources—your time and your money—arise.

You have less predictability in your schedule (babies who won't sleep or sick kids), more activities to plan for (more mouths to feed, play dates, extracurriculars), more personalities to deal with, and for most people, not as much solid sleep!

You also have lots of new expenses you've never had to plan for before; current expenses like diapers, bottles, new clothes every few months, more food, and childcare, as well as future expenses like sports, camps, and education.

Besides the huge change in your life of having kids to take care of, there is a huge shift in your priorities. Some people cope with this better than others, but no matter how prepared you are, it's a challenge.

Time Management

The less free time you have, the more planning your time becomes critical. Think about our discussion in Chapter 5 about planning out your week; when you're a parent, this kind of planning can be life-changing.

When you have a new baby, you're not sleeping and you're just getting to know your tiny human, this is less applicable. Planning is tough and can put unnecessary pressure on you when your body is healing and there are already a lot of emotions flowing. This period of time is all about recovery and survival.

As your baby gets into a little more of a routine, then grows into the toddler years and beyond, get out that calendar and start planning your time. Decide what is most important to you and your well-being and make time for it.

Decide how often/when you want to exercise, how/when you want to plan for your meals, how much sleep you need to feel your best, and what other time you need for yourself (and with your partner) to stay sane. If you're reading this and feeling like this is selfish, I truly understand. As a new mom, I've been on an emotional rollercoaster trying to figure out a schedule and do it all. Some things are more important than others, so plan for the big things—the ones that bring you the most peace and happiness.

Including some "me" time in your schedule is a necessity. This looks different for everyone, and may change over time, but to be the best parent and best partner, everybody needs some time just for themselves. You deserve that.

Keep this planning simple and consistent. Whenever possible, make meals the whole family can have, rather than planning different things for everyone. Find consistent time slots for exercise, errands, chores, time for yourself, and alone time with your partner. If this requires help from someone else (partner/grandparent/babysitter), it's much easier to make it happen when you've got a consistent plan!

Managing Your Money

With new expenses to deal with as a parent, having a grasp on your finances is nonnegotiable. Even if you felt like you had plenty of cash flow pre-kids to pay bills and get by, that's not good enough anymore.

There are many opportunities for impulse purchases when you are exhausted and desperate for your child to be comfortable and entertained. Additionally, there's the whole cute factor to deal with as you browse kids clothing sections—there are so many things you *need* because they're so darn cute. Spending can get out of control in a heartbeat, and it can stay out of control for a long time.

One of the things on your calendar needs to be time to look at your finances. If you have a partner, do this together, as discussed in Chapter 6. Spend half an hour each week until you fully understand where your money is going and have a clear picture of how to budget going forward, including any additional savings you can create for your kids' future. Revisit this once a month to see how things are tracking or anytime there's a new expense, such as a change in childcare.

As with all savings goals, automate the process. If you decide that, say, $100 each paycheck is going to your own savings and $50 is going to savings for your children, set that up to happen automatically, either through your employer or with your bank. Make the decision once, take a few minutes to set it up, and then you won't have to think about it again.

Rather than buying everything new for your kids, take any chance you get for hand-me-downs and used items. There are certain things like used cribs/mattresses and car seats that you don't want to risk because of possible recalls, but there are plenty of other expenses you can cut out completely or drastically reduce by accepting second-hand options. Clothes and shoes are sometimes worn just a couple of times or never at all. Things like toys, baby swings, bikes, and books are great second-hand candidates. Think outside the box and see what's available in your area before buying new. One example of this is Buy Nothing groups on Facebook, where you can ask for anything you're in need of and see if a neighbor may be able to help. With Buy Nothing, you can also get rid of things as your kids grow out of toys or clothes. Another example is an organization called Just Between Friends, which holds events periodically in various cities, for parents to both sell their own used items and buy from other parents.

Asking for Help

If you're used to doing everything for yourself, know that you physically cannot continue this habit when you have kids. I have such a deep-rooted need to be self-sufficient and independent so this has been one of the hardest things for me to accept. It takes daily effort.

If you're lucky enough to have friends or family who you trust, ask them for help—with the kids or other things like picking up groceries or doing laundry. Generally speaking, people like to feel needed and helpful. Doesn't it make you feel good when your loved ones ask you for help and you can offer it? This can, and should, go both ways.

You are not weak or incapable when you ask for help. You're human, and you're dealing with other little humans. It's good for everyone involved to have assistance from other sources when possible.

Chapter Summary

1. Becoming a parent changes your life, but it doesn't mean you can't or don't deserve to take care of your own needs anymore; when you're at your best, you'll be the best parent possible.

2. Make a schedule of how to spend your time, including meals, exercise, sleep, and free time (even if that's just 10 minutes).

3. Budget for expenses related to your children; these can quickly get out of control. Always consider second-hand or free options, rather than buying everything new for your kids.

4. Ask for help. I know this can be hard, but practice it daily, even if it's asking your significant other to help for 15 minutes while you take a shower in peace or asking a neighbor to grab something for you at the grocery store.

CHAPTER TEN

Lighting the Fire

I often have people ask me how I maintain motivation to be active, eat healthy food, and stay on top of my finances. They say that they know exactly what they need to do to achieve their goals but they just lack motivation. You know what my response is?

You can't wait for motivation. I'm not always motivated either! The ultimate goal is to create ingrained habits that make motivation unnecessary. Until you have those habits in place, you need another way to light the fire inside you when you're feeling unmotivated.

Create a scenario in your head that you can revisit when you're doubting the importance of your health. Look back at the exercise you completed in Chapter 4 and your "why" that you defined in Chapter 5 to get your mind in the right place.

This scenario can be something like being in a beautiful, tropical vacation spot and not being able to get in the water due to physical limitations. Or the image of not being able to run around the park with your children. Compare that to an image of you playing your favorite sport tirelessly, or watching your kids wear out before you do. Find something that resonates with your life and what you find important.

Unfortunately, no one can guarantee that if you live a healthy life—eat nutritious food, move your body regularly, get sufficient sleep, and stay hydrated—you will never deal with health concerns. Obviously, we all get sick from time to time. There's no escaping that. No matter how well we treat our body, things can happen such as accidents or disease. But the point is to do all things that *are* in our power to allow our body to function at its best.

Find a scenario in your head that you can revisit when you're struggling to follow through on your financial goals. Look at the exercise you completed in Chapter 4 and your "why" that you defined in Chapter 6 to get your mind in the right place.

This scenario might be an image of you sitting in a dingy room, mulling over a pile of outstanding bills and wondering how you're going to pay them all. Compare that to an image of you and your loved ones enjoying time in your dream home, stress free. The comparison, whatever it looks like for you, should light a fire inside to help you through the tough days.

Find words and ideas that inspire you. Keep them in front of you; keep sticky notes on your bathroom mirror, next to your bed, in your car, or on your phone. Read them out loud anytime you see them. I've even made a cheat sheet of some of my favorite phrases you can download and print to get started here: https://tinyurl.com /GYSTdailyaffirmations.

Then, once something is a habit—a real habit that is second nature, you just do it. You don't think about whether the workout will happen. You don't think about what the best meal choice is. You don't think about whether you're going to save money this month. You just do it!

You'll still have the inevitable excuses come up, like:

- I don't feel like eating vegetables.
- It's so boring to think about my budget—I just want to have fun.

- I work hard for my money, so I deserve to spend it however I want.
- I don't have time to make food or exercise.

But the excuses are quickly pushed aside once your habits are in place. You literally take all the energy out of the decision-making process, and you just do it!

No matter how you're feeling emotionally, commit to baby steps right now.

Chapter Summary

1. Motivation will come and go; the goal is to build habits that are so solid they don't require thought.

2. As you work toward building these habits, have scenarios in your mind that support why you are working on these habits. Daily affirmations that you say out loud will help with your mindset.

CHAPTER ELEVEN

Don't Expect Perfection

You may not realize this, but by implementing the steps I've outlined in this book, you're embarking on a life-changing and emotional journey.

Making big changes in your life can be a rollercoaster. When you initially commit, it might be really exciting and invigorating. You will feel a super "high" as you implement new practices and start seeing results. This emotional high is amazing! You will feel unstoppable. It may last a week, a few weeks, a few months, or longer. Eventually, though, a rough patch will come up. This is reality. When you're working on a long-term plan—meaning a forever plan—it won't be all rainbows and unicorns. Eventually, bumps in the road will happen. Something that jars you emotionally, such as a break-up, change in job, family situation, or an unexpected expense. Something may throw you off your normal routine, like having to work more hours, travel for work, or care for a family member. Or something may happen in your life where you suddenly just don't feel the same level of excitement or willpower that you did before. In fact, you'll probably experience all of these things throughout your life. It's part of the journey.

As these arise, it's easy to slip back into old habits, to tell yourself that you just can't handle the "stress" of workouts, eating right, or spending time thinking about your finances. It's easy to tell yourself that today, you'll forget about all of those things and restart tomorrow (or next Monday).

When we are presented with road bumps, we can get down in the dumps and let disappointment derail us completely. Or, we can acknowledge that we are going through a tough time and tell ourselves to keep pushing through, knowing that whatever we're dealing with isn't permanent.

I've been in that situation many times. I'm in it right now with my daughter and her sleep habits. Ugh, it pains me as I write this, but we got into a good routine but then I let us slip back into old routines for too long, rather than nipping them in the bud. I'm also in it right now under COVID-19 quarantine with some food habits. The anxiety and boredom get the best of me at times. Snacking is so easy, especially when we can't go anywhere and our cupboards are far fuller than normal.

But, here I stand. Do I wish I was in a better place with my daughter's sleep habits? Yes! Do I wish I was doing a better job of controlling my snacking? Yes! I can wish those things as much as I want to, but that's not where I am today. So, what should I do now? What should you do when you're feeling this way?

When we are presented with these road bumps, we have two choices. We can get down in the dumps and quit. Or we can let disappointment derail us completely. We can tell ourselves, *See, I knew I couldn't commit to this. I was right and I just can't do it.*

Or, we can acknowledge that we are going through a tough time and take a stand, telling ourselves I am strong and capable and will keep pushing through; I know that what I'm dealing with isn't permanent. We can let ourselves feel disappointment, failure, or that we aren't worthy of reaching our goals.

These are all valid feelings. Don't reject them. Feel them in your body and let them move through you. Don't keep them inside; get them out. You know the saying, "When the going gets tough, the tough get going." This is exactly what I mean here. Know that the feelings you're having are temporary. You have the power to push through the yucky stuff and return to the new normal of taking care of yourself. This is where you can shine. This is where you can show yourself that you're worth everything you've ever wanted. Revisit your why and feel all the emotions and energy that come along with the vision and the amazing goals you have for your life. This should make you smile and feel joyful. Allow yourself the disappointment you experienced, but then get back to doing the things that make you feel good.

Perfection isn't even a word to entertain when it comes to life. Ask any "expert" you know in the health or finance arena or in any field. I assure you, every single one of them have personally experienced feeling like they've taken steps backward in their fields of expertise. We are human, after all. How fun would life be if nothing bad ever came up, anyway? It would be boring! The highs we feel wouldn't have any meaning if there were never any lows. So, embrace it all.

As long as you expect perfection from yourself, you will constantly be disappointed. The sooner you can give yourself permission to be human, the sooner you'll find the consistency you need to make slow and steady progress forward for the long-term.

Chapter Summary

1. At the beginning of anything new, excitement and adrenaline carry you through. Eventually, challenges come up and the excitement starts to wane.
2. Be prepared for these challenges. They are normal. Accept whatever emotions you feel and recommit to the vision for your life.
3. *Consistency* is the goal, not perfection.

CHAPTER TWELVE

Kindness to Our Planet

While writing this book, I got really focused on being kinder to our environment by reducing my personal waste, which turned out to benefit my health and finances as well. How?

Health-wise   As I started making small changes to cut back on trash and even recyclables, I noticed some other effects. By buying fewer packaged foods, I was naturally pushed toward healthier foods. Generally speaking, the only foods that come without packaging are fresh fruits and vegetables. You may also be able to find proteins and whole grains with little to no packaging, depending on where you shop. I've become very educated on where to find the best bulk goods, which has been a lifesaver for me. But snack foods, like chips, crackers, trail mix, cheese, candy, cereal, even bread, **all** come in some form of plastic packaging. By avoiding packaging solely for the purpose of being kinder to our environment, you end up buying healthier foods. It's a win-win.

Financially   Changing habits to be more environmentally friendly naturally made me save *money*! I now buy fewer "things" for our household and for my personal care. I also use less of the things I still do buy.

Let me share some specific examples. Take food, since we have discussed a lot about nutrition already. If you stop buying so many snack foods or buy them from a bulk goods section of the store rather than being forced to buy whatever size package the manufacturers decide is right, you will be shocked at how much less you consume. You'll find that you don't have your pantry stuffed full with so many snacks! You just buy the things that really sound good to you.

Additionally, when you start making more of your own food at home (because you're not buying ready-made meals as often), you can save money on some of your favorite meals. I personally love salads—I can eat them every day. When you're dining out, salads can cost a pretty penny and not even be very wholesome. I can't bear paying $10 to $15 for a bowl of lettuce with a couple of carrots and a few tomato slices on top. No thanks. I can easily make delicious and filling salads at home for more like $3 to $4 a serving. Apply this same concept to one of your favorite meals and I bet you can save money making it yourself.

I bought the book *101 Ways to Go Zero Waste* by Kathryn Kellogg and it was eye-opening, but common sense. It goes through areas of our lives and how we can simplify, which leads to making less waste. For household items like cleaning products, what we actually need to clean the house is very basic. Do you need a different cleaner for *every* surface in your house? Nope! You can use the same thing (or maybe two or three different things) to clean your bathroom, kitchen, floors, windows, etc. You don't need a cleaner for the kitchen, a cleaner for the wood floors, one for the tile floors, a different product for the shower doors, and yet another for the shower walls. You can get totally out of control with cleaning stuff. It adds up in terms of plastic waste, chemical waste, and money down the toilet (no pun intended).

The book also has cleaning product "recipes" if you want to give them a try.

Personal care items are an area that can be easy to tackle and reduce our waste, probably significantly more so for women. Take a look at all the personal care items you own—shampoo, conditioner, soap, hair products, face products, nail products, lip products, body lotions, etc. There are a lot, right? So many things! Do you use them all? Did you even remember that you had them all? I'm guessing 99 percent of you will say *No* to both of those questions. Just on that basis alone, there is room to get rid of clutter, waste for our planet, and unnecessary spending.

Chapter Summary

1. Eating more unprocessed foods, which tend to come with little or zero packaging, can reduce waste and any negative impact on the environment.
2. Working on our finances and cutting out unnecessary purchases reduces waste and any negative impact on the environment.

Our planet thanks us each time we make a choice that is better for her existence.

CHAPTER THIRTEEN

Time to Get Started

That's it. You're done with this book. Now, it's time to get started! I'd love it if you'd grab the notebook you've been using to take notes and jot down thoughts while you've been reading this and look over those notes. Remind yourself about the *why* we discussed; *Who Do I Want to Be?* from Chapter 4, and look at the steps I outlined in Chapters 5 and 6 about implementing changes to better your health and personal finances. If you don't take action, this book is just a bunch of words.

It's easy right now to put the book down and take some time for reflection. Maybe you'll share some of these ideas or warm fuzzy feelings with your loved ones, telling them how you just read a book that's going to support you in making changes you've wanted for so many years. Then you'll say *I'm going to start all these new habits Monday.*

That's all well and good and I definitely want you to soak up any positive emotions you're experiencing right now. I know from reading other people's books that the high you can feel when you suddenly have hope for yourself and feel energized to make changes is phenomenal! It's a high that makes you feel invincible. Please let those feelings energize you. But, also sit down and make a plan for yourself to start immediately—not Monday, unless Monday is tomorrow. It's amazing how quickly emotions can fade and lose their strength. It's also amazing how other people in your life, even people who truly love you and want the best for you, can be less than supportive of new ideas you have.

Gaining better health and personal financial stability is priceless.

I discussed the importance of sharing your plans for change with your loved ones, rather than trying to go solo and hide what you're doing. Discussing your desires for change with the people closest to you is essential for your success. However, I want you to be prepared: some individuals may initially give you some pushback or roll their eyes. It's okay! The pushback is about THEM, not about YOU. Sometimes people are threatened at the thought of you making changes, because of their own insecurities or fears around change. You're strong enough to take that on the chin and keep moving forward. The emotions of others have nothing to do with your goals and the vision for yourself. You know what you want for yourself and you're going to go after that. Starting now.

Better health is priceless. When you fuel your body with good nutrition, move it on a regular basis, show yourself how strong you are mentally and physically, and consistently work on your mindset, you're going to feel electric. You'll have more energy than ever before. You'll have confidence that's through the roof. You'll wake up excited to be alive. You may also experience amazing new opportunities and welcome new people into your life. As your attitude and outlook on life improve, your new energy, or aura, attract different things. And you're going to feel so good that you can take on these new things with vigor. That's the whole point of working on your health and well-being. Having a healthy mind and body isn't about being able to say *I'm so healthy*; it's about being able to live the kick-ass life you want. Without your health, you can't do all the things you want to do.

Financial stability is priceless. Besides making better use of your current cash inflow, you're going to be in a position to reduce stress from worrying about money. This, in itself, is worth so much. We have enough things to stress about, so let's save that stress for the things we don't have control over. You can have control of your personal financial situation if you carve out a little time in your schedule to implement what I outlined in this book. Do the work upfront and reap the rewards for the rest of your life.

My one wish for you is to make the most of your time here on earth. Take care of your body, take care of your mind, take care of your business (your personal financial situation *is* your business), and then enjoy the amazing life you were gifted!

Connect with me on social media for community and continued support on your journey.

Instagram: @healthcreateshappiness

Chapter Summary

1. You've finished reading and now it's time for action; go back and complete the exercises in the book if you haven't already. Look at Chapter 4, "Who Do I Want to Be?" Chapters 5 and 6 for evaluating your beliefs, and Chapter 6 for expense tracking. You can also download a one-page planner to walk you through those actions https://tinyurl.com/GYSTactionplan.
2. Right now is when you move forward or stay where you are. Take small steps every day.

This is *your* life; you are the creator. Know who you want to be and make choices that align with that vision.

Quick Reference Guide

Healthy Living
- Eat real (unprocessed) food
- Move your body every day
- Sleep enough (7–8 hours a night)
- Drink water

Finances
- Track your expenses for one month
- Analyze what you're spending and whether you're comfortable with each category
- Decide where you can cut spending—look at discretionary spending and expenses; focus on keeping what you get the most enjoyment from and eliminating the other expenses
- Commit to saving monthly; start small, say 5 percent of your income, and build from there

Made in the USA
Las Vegas, NV
02 October 2021